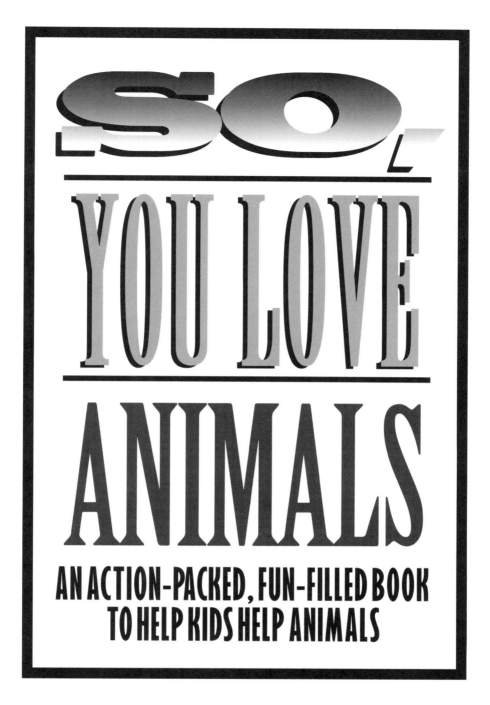

SO, YOU LOVE ANIMALS

AN ACTION-PACKED, FUN-FILLED BOOK TO HELP KIDS HELP ANIMALS

BY ZOE WEIL

Illustrated by John R. Gibson

D1122250

Acknowledgments

This book has had many readers who have offered invaluable suggestions and ideas. Abby and Carrie Lang, age eight and fifteen at the time, read the book in its first incarnation in 1990 and gave me the young person's critique. Elisabeth Anderson, Edwin Barkdoll, Sally Clinton, Peggy Eldon, Melissa Feldman, Jon Schottland, Dean Smith, Juliet Sternberg, Elizabeth Stevens, Julie Tamler, Denise Wright and Laura Yanne helped me to improve the book immeasurably through their careful readings. Special thanks go to Elaine Walton, who read and edited *So, You Love Animals* several times and was its most thorough critic. I am deeply appreciative of her help in writing this book.

So, You Love Animals ...
An Action-Packed, Fun-Filled Book to
Help Kids Help Animals
Published by Animalearn, the educational division of
The American Anti-Vivisection Society, 801 Old York Road, #204,
Jenkintown, PA 19046-1685, USA

First Edition, 1994

© Zoe Weil

Illustrated by John R. Gibson

Cover and book design by
Harris Design, Inc.

ISBN 1-881699-01-3

Library of Congress Catalogue
Card Number: 93-09021

Printed on Recycled Paper
with soy-based ink

This book is written in loving memory of my father,
Stanley L. Weil, Jr., who once kissed a hippo on the snout,
and is dedicated to my son, Forest Samuel Barkdoll-Weil.
May he grow up in a world in which children learn
to treat animals with kindness and respect.

1 ## Purrs, Barks, Licks and Love
Animals Who Are Our Friends

2 ## Tricks for Kicks
Animals Who Are Used to Entertain

3 ## Furry, Fuzzy and Feathery
Animals Whom People Wear

contents

Message to Parents and Teachers

I am a humane educator. I spend most of my days teaching young people about animals and the environment. As an educator, my purpose is to awaken the minds and hearts of young people, provide information, introduce new ideas and encourage critical thinking. Yet, it would be irresponsible to share information about what is happening to the Earth and to animals without also letting children know what they can do to help. So, I have written this book for young people who wish to know what they can do to make a difference.

Children all over the world are learning to respect animals and the environment. They are studying endangered species in schools, questioning some modern uses of animals and becoming active to help make our world safer, cleaner and more compassionate. They are often worried about the world they are inheriting and saddened by the suffering and destruction that they see around them.

This book lets young people know that they can help save animals and the environment, and it provides specific ideas and games which are fun, practical and empowering.

The children who read this book will need your support. Some of the information may make them sad and angry, but with your help, they will likely feel excited and energized to take on the challenge of saving animals and the planet. We all need these young people, and they need us. Thanks for your help.

Message to Kids

Our world is filled with animals, from tiny insects to scaly alligators to slippery salamanders to feathery penguins to furry lions to people. We all live on a beautiful planet called Earth, each trying to stay happy and healthy and live as long and as well as we can.

Some of my favorite beings in the world are animals, like my dogs Maia and Beau and my cats Père (pronounced "pair"), Uba, Mish and Buddha. I love these friends very much. I also like other animals, like deer and raccoons, crows and ravens, bears and coyotes, cows and pigs, chickens and turkeys, even rats and mice. These animals have a lot in common with my dogs and cats and even with me! They have feelings and families, and they play and communicate with each other. Birds and mammals, and even some fishes and reptiles, care for their young, protect them, help them to grow up safely, and teach them how to live on their own, like human mothers and fathers do. These animals all have their own lives to live, just like us.

Humans aren't always good at sharing the planet with other animals. That's a shame because animals are quite good at sharing the planet with us. The problem is that the people who aren't good at sharing the planet with animals have made quite a mess of things.

That's where you come in.

If you're a kid who loves animals, this book is for you. When you read it you're going to learn a lot of amazing things about animals. You'll also learn some things that will make you feel angry and sad. That's okay though, because the best part about this book is that it tells you how you can help animals, which is really important.

It's also fun.

I have two young friends named Carrie and David. Several years ago I told them about some of the things that were happening to animals, and ever since then they've been very busy helping animals and telling their friends and even their parents. They've taught so many of their friends that there's a whole group of kids saving animals in their neighborhoods. That's pretty great.

Animals need help in every neighborhood, so I hope that you'll want to help animals, too. All you have to do is turn the page ...

... and then go save some lives!

Joining the Kid Animal Action Team

Helping animals is fun, but it takes a little effort. It's often easier to help animals if you have some friends who want to join you. You may be lucky; your best friend may want to help animals, too. Then again, you may have to ask around. The good news is that all over the world there are kids like you who want to help animals.

If you care about animals, you're invited to join the Kid Animal Action Team, KAAT for short (pronounced like "cat"). KAAT is kids helping animals, and there are a lot of ideas and activities for KAAT in this book. There are KAAT skits and plays, KAAT experiments and KAAT games. If you love animals, and you want to help them, consider yourself a member of KAAT! There are no membership dues, or anything like that. If you want to help animals you are a member of KAAT - it's as simple as that!

There are hundreds of activities and suggestions in this book to help you help animals. Some of them are easy; some are a little harder. The best thing to do is to pick the activities that feel right to you. If you do just a few things in this book, you'll save a lot of animals.

Let me explain some of the KAAT activities: KAAT skits will help you help animals by giving you practice talking to people and asking them not to hurt animals. KAAT plays will help you teach all your friends about what's happening to animals. KAAT experiments will show you cool things about animals. And KAAT games? Well, you'll find out about KAAT games.

You can do most things in this book alone, but you'll need a friend for some of the KAAT activities. It feels really good to have a friend who's part of KAAT, too, because sometimes it's hard to try to change the world all by yourself.

You may not know anyone right now who cares about animals the way you do. That's okay. If you're busy helping animals, it won't take long before you meet others who want to join you. If you have any questions about KAAT activities (or anything else in this book), or if you need help finding other kids in your area who care about animals, write to me, and I'll try to help you. My address is: Animalearn, 801 Old York Road, #204, Jenkintown, PA 19046-1685.

chapter

1

Purrs, Barks, Licks and Love

Animals Who Are Our Friends

I think that the best place to start helping animals is with animals who are our friends (like dogs, cats, rabbits and guinea pigs) because they're already the ones we know and love best. There's also a lot we can do to help them.

Animals can be really great friends. Sometimes animals can even be our best friends. And people can be really good friends to animals, too. Although sometimes we're not. If you want to be a good friend to animals just turn the page ...

... and then go save some lives!

Be a Responsible Animal Parent

Bringing an animal into your home isn't like bringing home a new television. If you got really mad and smashed the new TV your parents might send you to your room for what feels like forever, and you might wish you'd never even heard of a TV. You might feel pretty awful, but the TV wouldn't. The TV couldn't feel anything no matter how hard you smashed it.

Animals are a lot like people. If you get really mad and hit your dog, you're going to hurt her, and she's going to feel sad and afraid. If you forget to feed your cat, your cat is going to get hungry, and if you decide you'd rather go to a baseball game than clean out your hamster's cage, your hamster may feel miserable.

Animals need food, water, a warm, clean place to live, exercise, veterinary care and lots and lots of love!

People who bring animals into their home are responsible for them, just like parents are responsible for their kids.

Get Some Facts!

■ Dogs are descended from wolves. Wolf parents don't hit their pups; they don't even know how! Wolf parents do quite a good job of training their pups, though. Some people hit their dogs because they think that's the way to train them. That's silly. You never have to hit a dog to teach her. You'll learn more about training dogs later.

■ Antifreeze, which is a green liquid used in automobile radiators, is poisonous to dogs, cats and other animals. Some people put antifreeze in their car, and then leave the container on the street. The container may have a little bit of the antifreeze left in it. Antifreeze smells and tastes sweet to dogs and cats, and when they find some left on the street they may lap it up. Some of them die from eating antifreeze.

True or False?

	true	false
1. Mice, gerbils and hamsters need the same things to stay happy and healthy.	☐	☐
2. Cats and dogs don't get along well and should never live together.	☐	☐
3. Animal friends let us know what they need from us.	☐	☐

Answers to True or False Questions:
1. False. Mice, gerbils and hamsters may all be small, furry rodents, but they have different needs and requirements. For example gerbils and mice are social animals. That means they like to live with other gerbils and mice. Hamsters, however, usually like to spend most of their time by themselves.

2. False. Some cats and dogs don't like each other very much, but many cats and dogs live together very peacefully. Sometimes they even become good friends. If you bring a cat into a dog's house, or a dog into a cat's house, it is important to let the animals have their own separate places and get to know each other slowly.

3. True and false. Our animal friends are usually pretty good at letting us know when they're hungry, or when they need to go for a walk, and sometimes when they're sick, but they can't speak English, and they can't tell us when it's time to go to the veterinarian (or vet for short), which is the name for an animal doctor. That means we have to pay a lot of attention to animals and learn how to care for them properly.

Some Things You Can Do to Be a Responsible Animal Parent

■ Before you adopt an animal, sit down with your family and think about the amount of time, money and energy you have for an animal. Once you know these things you can decide what kind of animal is best for your family. If everyone in the family is either at work or school all day, then a dog would not be a good animal to adopt, but adopting two cats might work out well since cats usually require less work than dogs and can also keep each other company during the day.

Studies have shown that people who live with animals often live longer than people who don't!

■ Before you adopt an animal, buy a book about the animal and read it carefully. It's important to know what animals need before you bring them home. You can also borrow books from the library, but it is best to have one good book to keep at home so you can look at it whenever you need to.

■ Choose each family member's job in caring for your animal. Who will walk the dog in the morning? in the afternoon? in the evening? Who will scoop the kitty litter? Who will pay the vet bills? Who will clean the gerbil's cage? Which parent is responsible for making sure all the jobs get done?

■ Remember: animals feel things just like you do. Before you do anything to an animal, ask yourself, "would I like that?" Chances are that if you don't like being teased, or having your ears pulled, or being hit, your animal won't like it either.

■ If you see a container of antifreeze on the ground, ask an adult to pick it up and throw it in the garbage for you.

■ Give your animal an extra rub right now to show how much you love her!

Be Your Dog's Best Friend

Did you know that dogs have rescued people from burning buildings and have found injured kids in the woods? Some lost dogs have traveled hundreds of miles to reach their homes.

There's one story about a dog who waited every day at a train station for her human to return from work. One day, the human didn't come home on the train. As it happened, he had died, but the dog had no way of knowing that. The dog waited at the train station for the rest of her life. Now that's loyalty!

Dogs give us lots of love. They comfort us when we're sad, protect us when we're in danger, play with us when we're lonely, warm us up when we're cold and make us laugh when we're mad. They don't care if our eyes are blue or brown, or if our hair is frizzy or straight. They like us just the way we are. We're pretty lucky to have such good friends.

You would think that any animal who gives so much love would get a lot of love back. But believe it or not some people don't treat their dogs very well: they leave their dogs outside by themselves all day and night, or forget to feed them, or decide not to give them a good walk because it's cold or rainy outside, or hit them when they're mad.

Get Some Facts!

■ A group of dogs is called a pack. A pack of dogs always stays together. They play together, sleep together, find food and eat together. Dogs who are left alone all day long get very lonely. They want to be with their pack of humans! That's why people who are gone from home all day shouldn't get a dog; they should only have animals who don't mind being alone for awhile.

■ Chocolate is poisonous to dogs and can make them sick.

■ Some people have their dog's tail or ears cut short to make them look a certain way. These operations are called tail docking and ear cropping, and they are unnecessary.

■ Dogs can hear much better than humans. Your dog can hear a prowler outside your house and wake up immediately even though you might sleep right through the noise. That's why so many people feel safe when they have a dog in the house.

■ Dogs like to know how to behave, so they need to be trained, kindly but firmly.

Some Things You Can Do for Dogs

■ You and your family can take your dog to obedience school to train her. Obedience school is fun for both you and your dog. You can find out about obedience school from your local Society for the Prevention of Cruelty to Animals (SPCA) or animal shelter.

■ Remember: never, ever hit your dog!

■ Brush your dog at least once a week. While you're brushing her, check for fleas, ticks and sores. Spread her toes apart and check her paws for burrs or splinters. Look inside her ears to check for dirt or mites (which will look like dark goo). Make sure not to poke inside her ears, though. If you see a problem, tell your parents right away.

■ Help your parents keep track of your dog's visits to the veterinarian. Your dog should visit the vet once a year for her vaccinations and whenever she gets sick.

■ Keep your dog on a leash when you're walking on the street. Even the most well-trained dogs sometimes run across roads suddenly if they see a squirrel, rabbit, or another dog.

■ How many of you knew sweating was cool? Well, it is! When people sweat we cool off. Dogs can't sweat like people. In order to cool off, dogs pant, but panting doesn't work as well as sweating, so dogs can get really hot and even die if they can't get out of the heat. Many dogs die every year because people leave them in hot cars. This simple experiment will show you just how long it takes for a car to get too hot for a dog:

How Long Does It Take to Heat up a Car?

You'll need:

- ☞ an outdoor thermometer
- ☞ a watch
- ☞ a pad of paper and a pencil
- ☞ a car
- ☞ a parent

1.
When you wake up in the morning on a sunny, spring or summer day, check to see where your family's car is parked. You're going to want it to be in the shade for a few hours.

2.
As soon as the air feels warm, ask your parents to park the car in the sun. Make sure that the windows are open just a little bit.

3.
Check your thermometer and write down the temperature.

4.
Then put your thermometer in the car and sit by the car (not inside the car!) with your watch.

5.
Wait ten minutes.

6.

Take your thermometer out of the car. Write down the temperature.

7.

How hot did the car get?

8.

Now ask your parents to move the car into the shade.

9.

Put the thermometer back in the car and wait for ten more minutes.

10.

Check the thermometer and write down the temperature.

11.

How hot is the car in the shade?

Learning from numbers: What did you notice? Was the car very hot? Was the car hot even in the shade? If the car got above 80 degrees, it was too hot for a dog. Now you know why it's dangerous to leave a dog in a parked car!

■ If you ever see a dog panting in a parked car when it's hot outside (especially if the car is in the sun), get an adult to help you call the police.

■ You can help dogs by getting to know them. The more you understand them, the better you'll know how to treat them. Have you noticed that when you come home each day, your dog seems to know that it's you coming up the path. Maybe she barks, or maybe she's already at the door when you arrive. She can hear you from far away, and she can recognize your footsteps.

Dogs have an amazing sense of smell, much better than a human's, but they could care less about the smell of roses. Sometimes they like smells that people think are gross.

Getting to Know Your Dog's Talents

When you come home from school, walk more quickly and heavily, or more softly and slowly than usual. Does your dog still recognize you and greet you at the door? Try this experiment by coming in a different entrance to the house, or walking toward the house from a different direction. Try this experiment for a few days. Soon your dog will learn all your tricks. Aren't dogs smart?

Be Fine to Your Feline

A lot of people have cats. Some people think that they own their cats, but the cats know better: cats probably think they own humans. You may have noticed that every cat has his own personality. Some are very pushy and want you to pet them all the time. Others are so independent they act as if they don't need you at all. For example, my cat Père has a very different personality from my cat Mish. Père wants me to pet him a lot. When I'm walking around the house he often runs in front of me and plops down on his back. If I ignore him and keep walking, he just does it again. He'll keep on plopping down in front of me until I pet him. Mish would never do that! That would be much too undignified for her. Mish acts like she doesn't want people to think she needs to be rubbed at all.

Some cats, like Mish, may act aloof (like they could care less about you), but deep down inside even the most aloof cat needs his human being. They may not need to be walked, and they're pretty good at exercising themselves when they need to (which isn't too often because a cat's favorite activity is often sleeping), but they do need their humans for some things. For example, cats like to stay very clean. They clean themselves everyday by licking every inch of their fur. But cats can't clean their litter box, so they need their human to do that for them. Sometimes cats need their nails trimmed, and sometimes they need to go the vet. Sometimes they just need to get rubbed.

Get Some Facts!

■ Cats knead people. When kittens are nursing (drinking their mothers' milk) they move their paws back and forth on either side of their mothers' teats in order to help get the milk out. This is called kneading. Some cats never outgrow kneading even when they're old. Since they don't knead their mothers anymore, some of them knead their people.

■ Cats need their claws for climbing and protecting themselves. Some people think that cats who live indoors don't need their claws. These people may have their cats' claws removed (which is called declawing). Cats can be sneaky though, and sometimes indoor cats get outside by mistake. Cats who don't have claws can't climb trees to escape dogs or other animals, and they can't protect themselves as well in a fight. You may think that declawing a cat is like trimming your fingernails, but it's not. It's like removing the top joint of your fingers where your fingernails grow! Even if you were given a drug to make you sleep while part of your fingers were cut off, imagine how much your fingers would hurt when you woke up. That's what it's like for cats who are declawed.

Some Things You Can Do for Cats

You don't have to declaw your cat, even if he scratches the furniture. Instead, you can build your cat a scratching post and train him to use the post instead of the furniture.

To build a cat scratching post you'll need:

- ☞ some old carpet scraps
- ☞ a thick cardboard barrel or tall box
- ☞ non-toxic glue
- ☞ a hammer and nails or a big, heavy-duty stapler
- ☞ an adult to help you
- ☞ a pillow the size of the bottom of the barrel or box

1. Turn the barrel or box upside down so the opening is on the floor.

2. Wrap the carpet scraps around the barrel or box and see how they fit best, then take the scraps off, remembering how they fit.

3. Put glue on the scraps and then press them onto the barrel or box.

4. Use the staples or nails to make sure the carpet stays in place. (You'll need the adult for this part.)

5. Put the pillow on the top (which is really the bottom since you turned the barrel or box upside down when you started).

Presto, you have a combination cat scratching post and cat lounge chair! Your cat will probably use his post right away, but you can encourage him by sprinkling catnip on the carpet scraps. (You can get catnip at a pet supply store, or grow it in your garden in the summer, or on a sunny windowsill.) Whenever your cat scratches the furniture, say "no" and gently pick him up and carry him to the scratching post. Hold his paws up to the carpet scraps and move them in a scratching motion. Your cat will soon figure out what he should and shouldn't scratch.

Chapter 1. Purrs, Barks, Licks and Love

■ Make safe toys for your cat. Cats like to bat small objects around, but some objects, like aluminum foil or balls of string, can be dangerous. Try giving your cat a ping pong ball with a small string attached. Or make a pillow for your cat and stuff it with catnip.

To make a catnip pillow you'll need:

☞ a 6 inch by 3 inch scrap of cotton cloth

☞ a needle and thread

☞ enough catnip to stuff the pillow

1.
Make sure that you don't let your cat in your room when you are making this toy or you'll never get it finished!

2.
Fold the cloth in half inside out to make a square.

3.
Sew together 2 sides of the cloth and about half of the third side so that you have a small hole. Use very small stitches. (If you don't know how to sew, ask an adult who does. Sewing can be lots of fun!)

4.
Turn the cloth right side out and stuff the hole with catnip until you have a plump pillow.

5.
Sew up the hole, and give your cat his new toy. He'll probably purr "thank you."

■ It's always best to keep your cats inside. Cats can get hit by cars if they wander outside. If you do let your cat outside, make sure he has a collar with an identification tag, and keep an eye on him so he doesn't go into a street. The collar should have elastic in it so it can stretch. Otherwise, your cat could choke if he gets caught on a tree branch. It's good to have a bell on the collar, too, so that birds and other small animals will hear your cat coming and get away before your cat gets them!

■ Before you and your parents enter a car, look underneath and tap the top of the car, to be sure there are no cats hiding. Sometimes cats curl up under the shade of a car in the summer or climb underneath warm engines in the winter. You wouldn't want to start a car until the cat has moved!

No one knows why cats purr, but it's not only when they're happy.

You Can Stop Pet Overpopulation

Brownie wagged his tail when I walked over to his cage. It was Monday afternoon, and I'd been away all weekend. We were both really happy to see each other. Neither of us knew what was going to happen that day.

I'd been working at the animal hospital for a couple of weeks after school, and Brownie had been in a cage the whole time. He was a scruffy, friendly dog with beautiful, dark eyes.

That morning, the veterinarian told me to bring Brownie upstairs because we were going to put him to sleep. I thought Brownie was going to have an operation or something, so I brought him to the operating room. Then the vet brought out a dark, glass bottle which said poison on it. All of a sudden, I had a very sick feeling in my stomach. I asked the vet what the poison was for. He told me it was for Brownie. I said that I thought he was going to put Brownie to sleep, not kill him, but the vet told me it was the same thing. I knew I was supposed to be working for the vet, but I couldn't help it - I started to cry. I asked the vet why he was going to kill Brownie, and he said it was because no one wanted him. He said that there weren't enough homes for all the dogs and cats in the world. He called the problem pet overpopulation.

Brownie was killed because of pet overpopulation. I think that we need to find better solutions to the problem of pet overpopulation than killing happy, healthy animals.

Get Some Facts!

■ Some people want a dog or cat who looks or acts a certain way. These people may choose a purebred or pedigree animal who is likely to have characteristics they want. Because people want purebreds, these kinds of animals are bred a lot. That contributes to the problem of pet overpopulation.

■ There's actually a very simple solution to the problem of pet overpopulation. Perhaps you can even figure it out yourself:

Suppose you set up a lemonade stand on the corner, and every day for two weeks you only sold half of the lemonade you made and the rest went bad. What would you do during the next two weeks? Make less lemonade, right? That's what we need to do with our animal friends. Since there are too many dogs and cats, we have to stop them from making so many babies. That's not so hard. Dogs and cats can get an operation to keep them from having puppies and kittens.

■ Whenever someone buys an animal from a pet store or from a person who has let their animal have babies, and whenever someone lets their own dog or cat have babies, they're adding to the problem of pet overpopulation.

■ Sometimes people decide that they can't keep their dog or cat anymore. Instead of finding a new home for their animal, some people just leave their dog or cat on the street. What do you think happens to animals left on the street? You got it. Some get hit by cars. Some eat poisons. Some get diseases. Some can't find any food or water. And some have puppies and kittens who don't have homes either.

Some Things You Can Do to Stop Pet Overpopulation

■ You can adopt a dog or cat from an animal shelter or SPCA instead of buying one from a breeder or pet store. If you adopt an animal, you'll make her very happy. But remember, dogs and cats are a lot of work. You and your family must have the time, energy and money to care for an animal.

■ Ask your parents to take your dog or cat to the vet for an operation that will prevent puppies and kittens from being born. The operation for female animals is called spaying, for male animals it's called neutering. Some vets do the operations for less money than others, so your family can ask around if you find the operation difficult to afford.

■ When your friends tell you they want to buy a fancy, pedigree puppy, let them know about all the homeless dogs who are waiting to be adopted. The dogs in shelters and SPCA's are just as nice as the dogs in pet shops. Shelters even have many of the same pedigree dogs as pet stores. There are also many rescue groups for purebred dogs, so if people want a specific kind of dog, they can always adopt one from the rescue group.

■ You can ask your teacher to invite someone from the animal shelter or SPCA to come speak to your class about pet overpopulation. Many shelter workers are happy to come and talk to kids. They may even show you a movie about the problem of pet overpopulation.

■ It's a lot of fun to be published in a newspaper! You might want to write a letter to the editor of your local newspaper about the problems of and solutions to pet overpopulation.

Be a Pet Overpopulation Detective

Find a dog in your neighborhood who is going to have puppies. Imagine that the dog will have six puppies in her litter, and half of them will be male and half will be female. Assume that each female will have a litter of puppies twice every year. If none of these dogs ever gets an operation to prevent puppies from being born, how many dogs will you have in 1 year? in 2 years? in 3 years? Now that you know, tell your friends!

Spay Talk

(You'll need one friend for this role play.)

Choose one person to be a neighbor who wants to let his dog have puppies. The KAAT kid's job is to teach the neighbor about pet overpopulation and to encourage the neighbor to take his dog to the vet for a spay or neuter operation. Remember, no one likes to be told what to do, so practice expressing yourself in a kind and positive way. Switch roles to let each of you have a chance to be the neighbor as well as the KAAT kid. Tell each other how you felt as the neighbor. Which suggestions worked best? Which worked least well? Keep practicing until you can convince anyone!

A Puppy Play

Write a play about pet overpopulation and get some friends to help you act it out. Learn your lines and practice your part. When you're ready, put on the show for your class, your neighbors, your family and your friends. You'll teach lots of people about the problem of pet overpopulation.

In the time it took you to read about the problem of pet overpopulation about 100 puppies and kittens were born in the United States! In the same amount of time, about 80 dogs and cats were killed because there were no homes for them.

Get the Rat Facts

Hamsters like to sleep all day and run around at night, and generally they like to live alone. Gerbils, on the other hand, will play all day with their friends. It's important to know these things.

How would you like it if you had to spend your whole life in a room with your worst enemy? That's what it must feel like for a hamster to have to live in a glass box with some other hamster she doesn't like.

And how do you like it if someone wakes you up in the middle of the night? Well, that's what it's like for mice when someone wakes them up in the middle of the day.

Hamsters, gerbils, rats, mice and guinea pigs may be little, but these little animals feel things just like big animals. They protect their babies and feed them milk, and they like to snuggle up and stay warm, and they get scared if someone grabs them suddenly or picks them up by their tails.

Get Some Facts!

■ Guinea pigs aren't pigs at all. Their name comes from the squeaky pig sounds they make.

■ When mice are born, they're tiny and pink, and they have no fur.

■ Hamsters, mice, rats, squirrels and porcupines have a lot in common. They're all rodents, with two long sharp teeth in the front of their mouths.

Match each animal with her place of origin:

guinea pig	Middle Eastern deserts
hamster	South America
gerbil	Europe and Southern Russia

Some Things You Can Do to Help Rodents

■ Learn about which animals sleep in the day and which sleep at night; find out which animals like company and which like to be alone. Once you know, you can make sure to respect their needs and wishes.

■ If you have guinea pigs, mice, rats, gerbils or a hamster, make sure that their cage is roomy, with places to crawl and hide, safe exercise wheels and fun toys. Keep their cage very clean, too.

■ It's best not to let your animals have babies, because you probably won't have room for all of them. You might think that you can just give the babies to friends and neighbors, but you need to make sure that your friends will take as good care of the animals as you do. Not only do you have to find homes for the babies, you have to find good homes, and that's not always easy. So make sure that you don't keep male and female animals in the same cage!

Answers:
guinea pig - South America
hamster - Middle Eastern deserts
gerbil - Europe and Southern Russia

Help Your Hamster Build a Cloud House

Go with your parents to pick up some plain, white cotton balls at the drug store. Put three or four cotton balls in your hamster's cage in the evening. Your hamster may not do anything with the cotton balls until after you go to sleep, so check the cage in the morning. Put some more cotton balls in the cage the next evening. Your hamster will use the cotton balls to make a cloud house!

Hamsters have large pouches in their cheeks where they can hold and carry their food.

What's the Word on Birds?

Because birds are so pretty some people like to keep them as companions so they can look at them a lot. Many of the really colorful birds are captured in the wild before they wind up in pet stores. Once they're caught they're stuffed into little boxes and put on ships or airplanes. Sometimes it takes a long time to get to the pet shops. By the time they get there, most of them have died!

I usually feel sad when I see birds locked up in cages. Their feathers look pretty, and sometimes they chirp or sing nice songs, but they can't fly. If I could fly, I'd be pretty sad if someone locked me up in a cage for my whole life.

Get Some Facts!

■ Birds have hollow bones so that they won't weigh too much. A heavy bird wouldn't be able to fly very far.

■ Female birds lay eggs, but if there's no male bird around, the eggs won't be fertilized and will never hatch.

■ When someone says "you eat like a bird" they usually mean you don't eat much. When they say "you eat like a pig" they usually mean you eat a lot. Obviously these people don't know much about birds or pigs. Birds eat a lot of food because they need so much energy to fly, while some pigs are actually fussy eaters.

Some Things You Can Do for Birds

■ If you don't have a bird, think hard about whether you want to make a bird live in a cage his whole life, and make sure that you never get a bird who was caught in the wild.

■ Spend some time outside watching wild birds. Listen for geese honking as they fly overhead each autumn and spring. Watch hawks soaring above the trees, and hummingbirds hovering by a flower. Listen for rustling leaves to see songbirds flitting in and out of tree branches. There are lots of other ways to see birds in the wild, too. If you want to know how right now, flip to page 149 for some good ideas.

■ If you already have a bird, make sure you have a very big cage for him, with lots of perches, toys, bells, mirrors and treats. Give him fresh food and water every day. And make sure to keep his cage very clean.

■ If you have one bird living by himself, he can get very lonely. Talk to him, sing to him and play with him every day. Check the animal shelters, too, to find a bird to be a companion. (Make sure you adopt the same kind of bird.) That way, you'll help your own bird and a bird from the shelter.

- If you have other animals in the house, like cats or dogs, be certain that your bird is well out of their reach.

- If you let your bird out of his cage to fly around, keep the window shades lowered. When birds see windows, they think they can fly outside; they don't know about glass, and they sometimes fly right into the window and hurt themselves.

- Many birds like to have some peace and quiet at night, so you can cover their cage in the evening with a sheet. In the morning you can take the cloth off the cage and say "good day" to your bird.

Kid Hero

Ten year old Jeremy of Louisiana designed a poster showing people how animals should and shouldn't be treated. It was so well done that Jeremy won first place in a "Be Kind to Animals Poster Contest," and his poster was displayed for everyone to see!

Birds and reptiles have something in common: both have scales. Snakes and lizards have scales all over their bodies, though, while bird scales are only on their legs.

Give Your Best Wishes to Fishes

It's pretty hard for people to hang out under water to watch fishes. That's why people who wanted to watch fishes invented fish tanks. Sometimes people invent things that are good for them, but not necessarily for animals. Do you think that fish tanks are one of those things?

Some freshwater fishes from ponds and lakes can live awhile in fish tanks. Maybe the fishes don't mind swimming in circles all day. It's hard to know for sure. But there are other fishes, usually brightly colored, saltwater fishes from the ocean, who die very quickly in fish tanks. In order to get these fishes out of the ocean, people will sometimes put chemicals and drugs in the water which end up killing a lot of the fishes.

We need to make sure that we don't hurt any fishes just to put them in fish tanks. After all, the reason people keep fishes is because they like them, right?

Get Some Facts!

- Can you imagine breathing through slits in your skin instead of through your mouth or nose? That's what fishes do. They breathe through openings called gills on the sides of their bodies, and they breathe under water.

- Some fishes leap out of the water to catch insects for food.

- Some fishes glow, like fireflies.

- Coral reefs are being destroyed to capture tropical fishes to sell to people.

True or False?

	true	false
1. A shark is a fish.	☐	☐
2. A porpoise is a fish.	☐	☐
3. A starfish is a fish.	☐	☐

Some Things You Can Do to Help Fish

■ Visit ponds, lakes and the ocean and look into the water through goggles. See fishes as they are meant to be, swimming free!

■ If you already have a fish tank, keep it clean, and make sure you don't overfeed your fishes. Read books about fishes and learn which fishes can live together peacefully so that you don't put a new fish in the tank who might hurt or kill your other fishes.

■ Think really hard before getting tropical or saltwater fishes. Instead of filling a tank with fishes, you can fill a tank with soil or sand and place plants or shells inside. You can be very creative making a terrarium (instead of an aquarium!).

Fishes like to swim in schools! A school of fish is like a gaggle of geese, or a pride of lions, or a herd of cows. It's a word which means "group" or "crowd."

Answers to True or False Questions:
1. True.
2. False. Porpoises are mammals like us. They breathe air and feed their babies milk.
3. False. Some animals have confusing names, don't they?

■ You can go animal sleuthing! You can visit pet shops which sell fishes and be a detective. Look for crowded fish tanks, dead fishes floating on the top of tanks, tropical or saltwater fishes, fishes with sores on them or with parts of their tails chewed off. If you see any problems, write to the store manager about them. Writing letters is easy and fun. You get to express yourself however you want, and no one interrupts you! You can also call your local SPCA or humane society and ask to speak to the cruelty investigator. Introduce yourself and tell the cruelty investigator what you saw.

Supporting Shelters Not Shops

When I was a kid I used to pass a pet shop on my way home from school every day. I liked to stop in the store and play with the puppies. What I didn't know then was that a lot of those puppies came from puppy mills.

Puppy mills are places where sad, lonely dogs live in small cages and have to give birth to puppies over and over again. Every time the dogs have puppies, the puppies get taken away to be sold in pet shops. Pet shops usually sell purebreds, and puppy mills provide a constant supply for shops to sell. After about five or six years, the dogs in the puppy mills don't have enough puppies, so they're killed!

Chapter 1. Purrs, Barks, Licks and Love

Get Some Facts!

■ Many puppies in puppy mills are taken away from their mothers when they are much too young. Then they're put in little boxes and cages and may travel for several days before they get to the pet shop.

■ In many states, if you buy a puppy from a pet shop and your puppy comes home with a disease, the pet shop doesn't have to help you pay a vet to make her well.

■ If a puppy gets sick in a pet shop, the owner will sometimes kill her rather than spend the money to make her well.

■ There are other animals in pet shops whose lives are pretty crummy. Birds are sometimes kept in dirty, crowded cages, and mice are often piled up together in little tanks.

Some Things You Can Do to Help Animals in Pet Shops

■ Instead of buying an animal from a pet shop, consider adopting one from an animal shelter or SPCA. It's kind of funny to buy a living creature anyway, isn't it? If people didn't buy puppies from pet shops, then the puppy mills would go out of business, and the dogs in shelters would find good homes instead of being killed.

■ You can get out your magnifying glass and go animal sleuthing in your neighborhood pet shops. Look for sick animals and dirty cages. Look at the birds: are their cages clean, with lots of perches, toys and fresh, clear water, or are many birds crowded into small cages? Do the birds look healthy, or are their feathers chewed up? Are the birds caught in the wild or bred in cages? Are small animals like mice and gerbils crowded into little tanks? If you see any problems write to the manager or call the cruelty investigator at the SPCA and report the problems you saw.

■ You can buy kitty litter, toys, collars, harnesses and leashes from pet supply stores that don't sell animals.

Protect Your Animals

Have you ever seen a dog tied to a pole on the sidewalk? or left alone in a yard? or a neighborhood cat roaming around the street? You might not know this, but it can be really dangerous to leave your animals outside by themselves. They can get stolen.

A lot of people wonder why anyone would want to steal a dog or cat, especially when we have such a big pet overpopulation problem. You'd think there would be enough dogs and cats to go around without having to steal one who lives with someone else.

Unlike human babies who can see at birth, puppies and kittens are born with their eyes closed.

But dogs and cats aren't stolen because somebody wants a companion; most of them are stolen by people who want to make money by selling them to laboratories where they'll be used in experiments. It's hard to believe that anyone would steal a dog or cat to sell to animal experimentation labs, but it really does happen, more than you might think. We'll talk about animal experiments later. Right now the important thing to do is to protect your animals.

Get Some Facts!

■ Some people who answer advertisements for dogs or cats that say "free to good home" don't plan on giving the animals a home at all. They answer these ads so that they can get animals to sell to laboratories.

■ The people who want to sell animals to laboratories will pretend that they really want a pet when they answer an ad for an animal. They can be very sneaky and cunning to get the animals.

■ Even though identification tags are very important, they don't prevent animals from being stolen.

■ Small and medium sized, friendly animals are more likely to be stolen than big, aggressive animals, but people still need to be careful even if they have larger animals.

Some Things You Can Do To Protect Your Animals

- You can have your dogs and cats tattooed. A vet can put a permanent tattoo identifying your animals on their bellies. That way, if they are ever stolen and sold to a laboratory the experimenters will know that they belong to you, and they can return them. They'll check the number of the tattoo with a number on file at a "find-a-pet hotline." Call Tattoo-A-Pet at (800) 828-8667 for more information.

- Be careful about leaving your pets alone in the yard all day. Animals are usually stolen when everybody is away from home.

- You may want to write a letter to the editor of your local newspaper about this problem. Most people have no idea that their animals might be stolen for experimentation!

- You can look in the "classified" section of the newspaper to find the advertisements for pets that say "free to good home." If you want, you can call up the phone numbers and warn whoever answers that he or she has to be very careful about giving animals away to someone who may sell them to laboratories.

- If you see a dog tied up to a pole, you can wait for the dog's human to come back and let her or him know that dogs can be stolen. (Warning: Don't touch the dog while you're waiting. The dog doesn't know you, and he could bite.)

Set up a KAAT Watch

You can get together with other kids in your neighborhood and keep an eye on dogs who are left alone in yards and cats who wander outside by themselves. If you see anyone driving around and watching the animals, let your parents know, and warn your neighbors to keep their animals inside when they're gone for the day. Check the color and license plate of the car or van, too!

Don't Have "Pet Regrets"

Some animals just don't make good companions. They don't like living in cages or behind fences; they don't particularly like people, and they don't belong in people's homes. For example, polar bears like to swim in very cold water and travel for miles on big blocks of ice. I don't have to tell you that polar bears don't make good companions for humans. Neither do monkeys, or raccoons, or opossums, or squirrels or foxes. In fact, most animals aren't meant to live with people!

It is estimated that two million dogs and cats are stolen every year in the United States.

Get Some Facts!

■ Some pet shops sell animals, like monkeys, who shouldn't ever live in people's homes.

■ Some people want an exotic, wild animal to keep as a companion even though the animal doesn't belong in their home.

■ Even if someone rescues and raises an orphaned, wild animal, that animal should be let free when she's old enough to survive on her own.

Some Things You Can Do To Prevent "Pet Regrets"

■ You can leave wildlife in the wild! That includes frogs, toads, snakes, turtles and caterpillars.

■ Visit the woods and sit quietly under a tree. Listen and watch for wild animals, and enjoy them in their own environment.

Find Out Which Animals Don't Make Good Companions

(You'll need at least one friend for this game.)

Choose one person to be "it" and to think of an animal. The rest ask three questions about the animal in order to decide whether the animal would make a good companion. The person who's "it" reveals the animal? Who was right? Switch, and try again.

Care for Classroom Animals

There was a hamster who lived in my classroom when I was in third grade, and I liked to play with her a lot. I didn't realize that when I took her out of her cage in the middle of the day I was waking her up. One afternoon I picked her up, and she bit me. Her teeth dug into my thumb, and she wouldn't let go. I was really scared. I started shaking my hand to get her off. Finally, she fell off onto the floor. My thumb was bleeding so badly I got blood on everything. It was awful, and I felt pretty sorry for myself.

Some animals, like zebras and wild dogs from Africa, can never really be tamed, even if they are orphans raised from infancy by humans.

It wasn't until much later that I started to feel sorry for the hamster. She hadn't wanted me to wake her up, but what could she do? She couldn't exactly say "leave me alone, Zoe," so I guess she told me in the only way she knew how. And what did I do when she tried to tell me she didn't like to be woken up? I shook her onto the floor! That must have been far more scary for her than her biting was for me. When I realized this, I felt pretty bad about what I had done to the hamster. I hadn't been thinking about what the hamster wanted, only about what I wanted.

It wasn't just my fault, though. I was eight years old, and someone should have taught me about hamsters. I hadn't known the best way to treat them. In fact, no one in my class had been taught anything about hamsters!

Get Some Facts!

■ Grownups should teach kids about animals, but sometimes they don't. That means you kids have to do some serious thinking on your own to make sure you don't hurt animals by mistake the way I hurt the hamster.

■ Classroom animals need someone to take care of them on weekends, during holidays and all summer.

■ Sometimes everybody in the classroom tries to feed the animals. That's not good. Some animals, like fishes, die from too much food.

■ Sometimes the temperature in school gets very cold at night, and the animals get very cold, too.

■ Classrooms are pretty noisy places for animals, like hamsters, who need to sleep during the day.

Some Things You Can Do to Help Classroom Animals

■ Ask your teacher to teach everybody in the class all about any animals who live in the classroom.

■ Start an animal care group in your class. Your group can make sure that the animals are treated well and are given everything they need to stay happy and healthy.

■ Ask your teacher if your class can hang a bird feeder outside the window instead of getting an animal for the classroom. You can get a bird identification book for the classroom to learn which birds come to visit. You'll have to keep the feeder filled with birdseed all winter because the birds will become dependent on the food you give them. If you want to know how to build a bird feeder right now, turn to page 149.

Be a Cruelty Detective

We've probably all hurt an animal friend because we didn't know better, or because we were careless. You know that you need to make sure that you never hurt an animal because you're mad at her or because you're in a bad mood.

It's not just hurting animals by mistake that we have to worry about though, because believe it or not some people hurt their animals on purpose! Some people beat their dogs, or kick their cats or whip their horses. I know that seems incredible, but it's true. There are laws against being cruel to animal friends just like there are laws against being cruel to kids, but in order to enforce laws, you have to catch the people who are breaking them. That's where you come in.

True or False?

		true	false
1.	Laws require that people feed their companion animals.	☐	☐
2.	Laws require that dogs get a rabies vaccination from the vet.	☐	☐
3.	It's against the law to yell at your animals.	☐	☐
4.	It's against the law to kick or beat your animals.	☐	☐

Some Things You Can Do to Stop Cruelty to Animals

■ You can write or call your state senator or representative. Find out the names and addresses of your senator and representative by calling up "The League of Women Voters." (You'll find their number in the telephone book.) Ask your senator or representative to send you a copy of the laws against animal cruelty in your state. Read and study the laws so you understand what is and isn't legal. It may be hard to read the laws, because they're sometimes written in a complicated way, but it's important to know them in order to be a cruelty detective. You can ask your parents or teachers to help you read and understand them. You can also call the cruelty investigator, and ask whether something is against the law.

Answers to True or False Questions:

1. True.
2. True and false. Some states require rabies vaccinations while others do not.
3. False. But it isn't very nice to yell at them!
4. True. There are anti-cruelty laws in every state to protect animals from abuse.

■ You may have already called the cruelty investigator to report problems at pet shops. You can also report any cruelty to animals that you see on the street. For example, if you see someone kicking a dog, you can call the cruelty investigator. Let her or him know that you want to help stop cruelty in your neighborhood!

Most violent criminals have had a history of cruelty to animals!

■ You can get out your binoculars and look for cruelty. Whenever you spot an animal, look to see whether the animal looks well-fed and well-cared for. Watch for animals who limp, whimper or look unhealthy. If you suspect animal cruelty, you can call the cruelty investigator.

Kind Talk

(You'll need a friend for this.)

Pick one of you to be the KAAT kid, while the other is a friend or neighbor who is beating or kicking his dog. (You can use a ball or box to be the dog.) The KAAT kid should practice talking to the neighbor and teaching about kindness and compassion. When you're done, the "neighbor" should say what things made sense and helped him understand that kicking dogs is wrong. Switch roles and try again. If you see friends or people you know kick their dog, you can help them and the animals by teaching them about kindness.

chapter

2

Tricks for Kicks

Animals Who Are Used to Entertain

Animals can be fun to watch. That's why there are a lot of animals on TV, and animals in rodeos, circuses and zoos.

Have you ever wondered whether the animals in these shows really want to perform for people, or live in cages or be movie stars? If you really care about animals, it's important to ask those questions. And if you really want to help animals who entertain people, just turn the page ...

... and then go save some lives!

Be a Zoo Sleuth

When I was a kid I felt a little funny about zoos and aquariums. On the one hand I liked to see all the amazing animals, but on the other hand, I really hated to see them in cages and tanks. As I got older, I started to hear some pretty awful stories about zoos. I heard that some zoo animals and lots of aquarium animals had been captured from the wild, and that sometimes in order to catch one baby animal, the animal's mom and dad and sisters and brothers were all killed! I also learned that some animals in zoos were beaten and whipped.

Some zoos and aquariums are much better than others. Some give the animals lots of room and try to make their living areas look like the animals' natural habitats, like the forest, or the jungle, or the desert or the ocean (depending on what kind of animals they are). Generally, the bigger zoos are better than the small, traveling zoos, but even some of the big zoos and aquariums capture and hurt animals or put them in small cages that look nothing like the forest, jungle, desert or ocean.

Get Some Facts!

■ The ponies who are used for pony rides at zoos have to pull and carry hundreds of kids every day. Sometimes they're forced to pull carts with too many kids in them, and that can hurt the ponies.

■ Not too long ago, a big aquarium had four whales captured from the ocean to put on display in a big tank. Two of the four whales died shortly after. Dolphins and whales are often caught in the wild and taken away from their families in order to be in aquariums, zoos and sea parks.

■ On average, dolphins and whales don't live nearly as long in zoos, sea parks and aquariums as they do in the wild.

■ Some of the chemicals in the water in aquariums are bad for dolphins' and whales' eyes.

Some Things You Can Do to Help Zoo Animals

Be a zoo reporter. When you visit the zoo, take this list of questions with you and do some zoo sleuthing:

Questions for zoo sleuths:

1.

Are animals pacing or rocking, or acting bored or sad?

2.

Are animals in small, empty cages or in large areas which look like their homes in the wild?

3.

Are cages clean?

4.

Do animals look healthy?

5.

Are there a lot of baby animals?

6.

Are animals who sleep during the day, like bats or raccoons, in a quiet, dark place, or are they in a noisy, bright area?

7.

Do animals have hiding places so they can get away from the stares and noises of people?

8.

Are animals who like to dig, like prairie dogs, in areas with soft dirt, or are they on concrete?

■ Once you've finished being a zoo reporter, you can write to the zoo director and ask any questions you may have, like what happens to the baby animals when they get big, or why are some animals in cages that don't look natural, or where have all of the animals come from. If you've seen any problems, you can ask the zoo director to please fix them soon.

■ If your class ever goes to the zoo, you can ask your teacher to give each student a sheet of questions like these so that the whole class can be zoo sleuths.

■ You can avoid zoos which keep animals in small, barren cages.

■ Before going to a dolphin or whale show, think about whether the dolphins and whales belong in tanks. If you decide that these animals should not be taken from their ocean homes, consider whether you really want to support a dolphin or whale show with your money.

■ Take a good look at the ponies used for pony rides. Do they look happy and healthy with shiny hair and bright eyes? Ask the owner of the ponies where the animals live, and, if you can, go check out their stables with your parents. If you see any problems, call the cruelty investigator. And think about whether you really want to go on a pony ride.

Dolphins and whales are very intelligent, gentle and compassionate. They've been known to rescue drowning humans!

Kid Hero

Junior high school student, Suzi Eszterhaus of California, was a zoo sleuth. She recorded all the problems she saw in zoos all over the United States and even in other countries. Then she told the United States Department of Agriculture and several humane societies what she had seen, and they went out and made the zoos clean up their act.

Shall We Really Go to The Rodeo Show?

Rodeos may be fun for people, but they're no fun for animals. Calves are roped around the neck and thrown to the ground, and animals who are normally quite calm, like horses and bulls, are jabbed and hit and made very angry while some strange person tries to ride them. Is that the right thing to do to animals just to have fun?

Get Some Facts!

■ Leather belts, called "bucking straps" are tied tightly around the bellies of the horses and bulls at rodeos in order to make them so uncomfortable that they buck and thrash around.

■ The calves who are roped at rodeos often get hurt really badly.

Chapter 2. Tricks for Kicks

- Wild horses are happy grazing freely on grass and would much prefer to be left alone than be forced to be in a rodeo show.

- Rodeo animals are transported all over the country in cramped trucks just to perform for people.

Some Things You Can Do to Help Rodeo Animals

- If the rodeo comes to town, you don't have to go. By not paying for the rodeo, you're casting a vote. You're saying that you won't spend your money to support activities you don't believe in. You can write to the people who organized the rodeo and let them know what you think about hurting animals for fun. Some people have politely asked that the rodeo be canceled.

- You can write a letter to the editor of your local newspaper about rodeos and share what you think about them.

- If the rodeo comes to town, you can ask the cruelty investigator to look for problems behind the scenes, like animals in cramped, dirty stalls, or animals who have been whipped, shocked or beaten.

Horses were brought to America by Spaniards. Usually, we don't think of horses as wild, but there are now wild horses who roam in many parts of the United States.

Have a KAAT Showdeo

Put on a play with your friends about the Wild West from the animals' point of view. Have each person play an animal (like a horse being ridden during a shoot-out or a cow being rustled up by a cowboy) and speak the thoughts of the animal. Perform the show for your families and classmates!

Circling the Circus

Do you think that tigers really want to jump through burning hoops, or that elephants really want to balance on one foot, or that bears really want to walk on balls, or that monkeys really want to dress up like people and smoke cigarettes? Sometimes it's hard to know what animals really want, but I imagine that animals at the circus don't like living in tiny cages, or traveling all over the place, or having to do silly tricks for people.

Get Some Facts!

■ Lions are a lot like house cats. In the wild, lionesses often lie around most of the day with their families. It's only when lions get hungry that they go out hunting for food.

■ Sometimes circus animals are whipped in order to get them to do things like jump through burning hoops.

■ Some circus trainers burn the bottoms of bears' front paws so that the bears will balance on their rear feet. Their front paws hurt too much to put them down!

Elephants make sounds lower than humans can hear. They may use these sounds to communicate over long distances.

Some Things You Can Do To Help Circus Animals

■ You can help circus animals just like you help rodeo animals. When the circus comes to town you can tell the newspapers and the circus organizers what you think about forcing animals to do tricks for entertainment.

■ You can always call the cruelty investigator again and let him or her know that the circus is in town. Time to protect the animals!

■ A few circuses don't have animals. If those circuses come to town, you can encourage all your friends to go with you for some real fun.

Be an Animal Entertainer Investigator

Have you ever seen an advertisement for a greased pig contest, or a diving mule show or a wrestling bear match? The ads make the shows sound pretty fun. Fun for people anyway; not for animals!

Get Some Facts!

■ Diving mules are forced to climb steep planks up to a high diving board. When they get to the top, they can't turn around, so they have no choice but to fall into the pool of water way down below them.

■ People remove the claws and sharp teeth of wrestling bears so the bears can't hurt anyone too badly.

■ In greased pig contests, a bunch of baby pigs are released in a pen while kids run around and try to catch them. The pigs are very scared, and sometimes they get hurt badly when they're picked up by an arm or leg.

Some Things You Can Do to Help Animal Entertainers

- If any of these animal shows come to your town, think about whether you want your money to support them.
If not, don't go!

- You can write to the newspapers which advertise these shows and tell them what you think about the animal acts. If you want, you can even ask them not to advertise the shows. If you hear ads on the radio, you can do the same thing by calling the radio station.

- You can always call the people who are hosting the shows and ask them to cancel the animal acts.

- You can keep your investigative eyes open all the time by looking in the entertainment section of the newspaper regularly. Look out for pigeon shoots in the fall, holiday reindeer pageants in the winter, bunny sales in the spring, and boxing kangaroos in the summer. You can write letters, make phone calls and hold KAAT meetings to talk to your friends about what can be done.

A mule is the offspring of a male donkey and a female horse. Mules are unable to have young.

Is It Really Fun to Kill Animals With Guns?

Some people think that it's fun to shoot, trap and hook animals. Personally, I think it's kind of weird to kill animals for fun. Whenever I see someone prying a hook out of a fish's mouth and then throwing the fish back in the water, I wonder why anyone in the world would want to do that to a fish.

My dog Maia and I like to walk in the woods. In fact, it's one of our favorite things to do. But every autumn when we go into the woods we hear gunshots, and I get really sad. It's hard to enjoy our walks when I know that a deer is getting killed nearby because someone thinks it's fun to kill. I also get scared that some hunter might shoot Maia, thinking that she's a deer. It's not fair that Maia and I and the deer can't be safe in the woods.

Get Some Facts!

■ Practically all the public forests are run by a small number of people who hunt or who think hunting is okay.

■ Fishes have very sensitive nerve endings in their mouths and biting into a hook hurts them.

■ In nature, it is usually the sick and old animals who are killed by predators (animals who eat other animals) or who die during cold winters, but when hunters kill animals, they often shoot the biggest and healthiest animals instead of the sick, injured or old animals. That's bad for all the animals.

■ Some people say that we have to kill deer otherwise there would be too many of them, but most animals (including deer) stop having too many babies if there's not enough food to go around. Not only that, hunters actually kill predators of deer including bears, bobcats, mountain lions and coyotes. If they really wanted the population of deer to decrease, they would leave the predators alone.

■ Sometimes mother animals get caught in traps. Not only do the mothers die, but their babies also die when their moms don't come back to feed them.

Some Things You Can Do about Hunting, Fishing and Trapping

■ Think hard about whether you want to kill animals, even bugs, for fun.

■ You can put "no hunting, fishing or trapping" signs around your property to protect the animals who live near you. You can put these signs up even if you live in an apartment in the city. You can also ask your neighbors if they would like you to post their land, too. You'll be letting people know that some people don't think it's okay to kill for fun.

■ Go on a photography hunt. Here's how: go to the park or woods with your parents and friends and look for wild animals like deer or rabbits. If you find a spot and sit quietly, the animals may come to you! Enjoy seeing animals instead of killing them. Use a camera to take some pictures.

■ If you have friends who like to hunt or fish, ask them to imagine what it would feel like to bite down on a sharp hook or get shot by a gun when they're minding their own business in their own home. Invite your friends to join you on a photography hunt instead of a killing hunt.

■ Write to the governor of your state (you can find out his or her address from The League of Women Voters). You can ask your governor to choose someone who doesn't like to hunt to help manage the parks and forests. Tell your governor why!

■ Check out the "To Learn More" section at the end of this book. Groups like the Fund for Animals can help you help animals who are hunted, fished and trapped.

Kid Hero

When Maggie McCool of New Jersey was ten years old, she volunteered at a nearby wildlife refuge every autumn. Autumn is when the hunters would come and try to kill the animals at the refuge. It didn't seem to matter to the hunters that there were signs posted all around the property that said "No Hunting, Trapping or Trespassing." The hunters would try to sneak on the property and kill the animals anyway. Maggie and her family helped to patrol the refuge during hunting season to keep the animals safe.

Every year over one hundred people are mistakenly killed, and over one thousand are injured, by hunters who aren't careful about whom they shoot!

Really See . . . What's on TV

Watching TV can be fun, but it's not necessarily fun for the wild animals who are used in commercials and TV shows. People who advertise products on TV think that using animals in commercials will help sell everything from clothes to cars to sodas. That's why when you turn on the television you may see chimpanzees wearing diapers and mountain lions lying on cars. Did you ever wonder how those animals got into acting as a career? Well, they didn't fly over from Africa or South America to try out for the part, that's for sure.

Get Some Facts!

■ A lot of the animals whom you see on TV are wild animals. In order to get wild animals to drink soda, or lie on cars, or walk on leashes you have to train them, and sometimes the trainers whip and beat the animals, or don't feed them enough.

■ When wild animals on TV get too old, or if they become too dangerous, they may spend the rest of their lives in small cages. Sometimes people just kill them when they're not useful anymore.

■ The chimpanzees you see on TV shows and in commercials are young, usually under six years old. Chimps who are much older than that get too big and dangerous to be used anymore. Sometimes they're sold to laboratories when they're too big for TV.

Some Things You Can Do
To Help Animal Actors

■ Be a TV detective. Keep a pad of paper and a pencil next to the TV. Anytime you see an animal on TV jot down a note about what you saw. You can include this information:

1.

The kind of animal.

2.

What the animal was doing.

3.

The name of the show or advertiser.

4.

The TV station.

5.

The date.

■ If you see a companion animal whom you think was mistreated, or if you see a wild animal who probably shouldn't be on TV at all, you can write a note to the producers of the show and let them know that you are very upset by what you saw. You can send the letters to the producer of the show and address them "care of" your local TV station. (You can find out the address of the TV stations by looking in the phone book.)

■ If you see a TV show about people helping animals, you can write to those producers to thank them. They like to know that you kids are out there appreciating their good shows.

- If you watch TV, try watching with a friend. Every time one of you sees a scene with an animal, talk about the scene and decide whether or not you think it was okay. If you don't think it was okay, you can write to the producer together.

- If you keep seeing animals hurt on a certain TV program, let the producers know how it makes you feel to see the animals hurt.

How to Be a Movie Detective

Animals are used in movies just like they're used on TV. Sometimes the animals in movies are treated well, and sometimes movies actually help animals by teaching people about some of the things that are happening to them. *The Bear* is a good example of a movie which helps animals. In some other movies, though, animals are treated really badly. If you ever see a western or an old war movie, you're likely to see horses who are stunned, knocked over, tripped, shot and even killed. Even though movies are make-believe, and the human actors almost never get hurt, the animal actors often get hurt. Sometimes it's hard to tell if the animals are really getting hurt. That's why you have to be a good movie detective.

Chimps are the closest living relatives to humans. 98% of their genetic material is the same as human genetic material!

Get Some Facts!

- The United States has laws to protect the animals in movies from being killed while the movie is being filmed. The laws don't protect the animals from cruel training before the film, or from harsh handling after the film, though.

■ If the movie is filmed in another country, then American laws don't help the animals. In many countries it's perfectly legal to hurt or kill animals in films.

■ Some animal organizations try to protect animals used during films. Unfortunately, they can't keep an eye on animals in all the films.

Some Things You Can Do to Help Animals in Movies

■ Be a movie detective. Being a movie detective is just like being a TV detective, except that it's a little harder to take notes in a dark movie theater. If you're a movie detective, you have to keep your detective eyes alert during the whole film. That's hard to do, because it means that part of you is not paying attention to the story, because you're paying attention to the animals.

■ If you think that an animal was hurt during a film, you can write to the manager of the theater. Let the manager know how you feel about animals getting hurt just to entertain people. If you want, you can ask the manager to please stop showing the film. If enough people ask, the manager may listen.

■ If you see a movie that says it's okay to hurt animals (like a movie about how great it is to go hunting or fishing), you can write to the manager about that, too.

■ If you know that animals are hurt in a movie, you can also write to the producers of the movie. (You can ask the manager of the theater to tell you the address.)

Orangutans are always moving from place to place in the forest. Practically every night they build themselves a new nest in the trees to sleep in.

Get on the Track About Racetracks

Horses and dogs may like to run, but that doesn't mean they want to run all the time, especially not if their legs hurt, or if they're tired or not feeling well. They don't have much choice though because people make racehorses and racing dogs run all the time.

It's bad enough when people make you do something you don't want to that's good for you, but when people make you do something that can be bad for you that's awful. That's what happens to racehorses and racing dogs.

Get Some Facts!

■ A lot of racehorses are given drugs so they'll run even when they're hurt.

■ Dogs are often trained to run fast by chasing cats or rabbits.

■ When the dogs and horses get older, or if they're not running quickly, they're often killed.

■ Horses are sometimes forced to race when they're much too young.

■ Racing horses and dogs get hurt. Sometimes they fall and break their legs or sprain their ankles. Often they're killed if this happens.

Chapter 2. Tricks for Kicks

Some Things You Can Do To Help Racing Dogs and Horses

■ Decide if you really want to go to the racetracks. Remember that your dollars cast a vote for what you believe in.

■ Usually, dogs who are used for racing are greyhounds. In order to save a greyhound from being killed when she can't race any longer you can adopt one. Learn everything you can about greyhounds and talk to your parents about adopting one. If you have the time, money and energy for a dog, consider saving a greyhound's life. Write or call Make Peace With Animals, Inc., P.O. Box 488, New Hope, PA 18938 (215) 862-0605 to find out about adopting a greyhound.

■ There aren't too many people who can give a horse a really good home, but if your family has the land, money and time for a horse, you can save a racehorse from being killed. You can write or call Make Peace With Animals, Inc. (they're the same group who'll help you adopt a greyhound), and they'll help you adopt a racehorse.

Because some greyhounds are trained to run quickly by chasing rabbits or cats, many of them can never live peacefully with cats. Many greyhounds are very friendly with other animals though, especially people.

■ You can write to the manager of a nearby racetrack and ask what happens to horses and dogs who get hurt or who can't race anymore. If you find out that the horses are sold at auctions and killed, you can write a letter to the editor of your local newspaper just like you did about the circus. You can also let your friends and family and teachers know about what happens to horses.

A KAAT-racing Skit

(You'll need a few friends for this role play.)

You'll need someone to play the horse, the jockey (that's the person who rides the horse) and the audience. If you have enough people you can also have other horses and jockeys. Have your own horse race, put the horses in their stalls, have the horses grow up - play out a bunch of different scenes. Then have the horses talk about how it felt to be racehorses. Switch roles so that everyone has a chance to play a horse. If you want to, put on a play for your friends about racehorses.

Don't Force the Carriage Horse

If you live in a city, or if you've visited a city, you've probably seen horses pulling carriages filled with tourists. The horses have to walk in the street in lots of traffic and breathe car fumes. Yuck. Next time you see carriage horses look into their eyes. How do they look?

Get Some Facts!

■ Some cities have no laws to protect carriage horses. That means that the carriage horses have to work even during rush hour, when everybody is going to or from work, and the roads are really crowded with cars.

■ "Blinders" are put on either side of the horses' eyes so they can only see straight ahead. The blinders are supposed to prevent the horses from being scared by cars coming up quickly alongside of them, but imagine how scary it must be not to be able to see cars or people coming up right next to you!

■ Some carriage horses have to work no matter how hot it is outside. Sometimes they get so hot and tired they faint and fall down in the middle of the street. Sometimes they even die from the heat.

■ Carriage horses breathe the exhaust fumes from cars, and sometimes they get hit by cars, too.

■ Walking on city streets can hurt horses' hooves and legs.

Some Things You Can Do to Help Carriage Horses

■ You can call or write to the mayor of your city, and say that you'd like to know the laws protecting carriage horses. Once you know, you can be a carriage horse cop! If the law says that horses should not be on the streets if the temperature is above 90 degrees, then you and your family can get your outdoor thermometer on hot days to check the temperature. As soon as it's 90 degrees you can let the police know it's time to ask the carriage horse drivers to call it a day. Of course, if there is no law to protect the horses, you can ask the mayor to help pass one.

■ Go animal sleuthing: politely ask a carriage horse driver where the stables are for the carriage horses. Ask your parents to take you there so that you can see how the horses are treated. Are the stables and stalls clean? Do the horses have enough room? Do they look like they've been brushed and groomed? If you see any problems, call your friend the cruelty investigator.

The world's first horse lived a long time ago and was smaller than many dogs.

Tourist Talk

(You'll need one friend for this skit.)

Choose one person to be the KAAT kid and the other to be a tourist riding in a carriage or about to get in a carriage. Practice politely asking the tourist to take a walking tour of your city. (For example, you might say: "Hi, I hope you're enjoying your visit, but how about walking and letting the horse have a break!") Switch roles so that each of you can practice being the KAAT kid. How does it feel to ask people to help out the animals?

Fight Animal Fighting

Some animals, like dogs and roosters, are forced to fight each other while people watch and bet on who will win. A lot of times the animals have to fight until one of them dies! That's one of the cruelest things I've ever heard of.

Get Some Facts!

- Making dogs fight each other is illegal, but it's done anyway.

- Pitbulls are the kind of dogs usually used for dog fighting, but pitbulls aren't born vicious and mean. In order to make dogs fight, people may beat them and scare them and try to make them really angry.

- In cockfighting, roosters have sharp, metal spurs strapped onto their legs so that when they fight each other with their feet, they'll cut each others' bodies.

Some Things You Can Do to Stop Animal Fighting

■ If you ever hear about dog fighting in your neighborhood, tell the police right away. Remember: dog fighting is illegal, and the police will stop dogfights. Don't try to stop the dogfights yourself!

■ In a few states cockfighting is still legal. You can call the cruelty investigator to find out if it's legal in your state. If it is, you can write to your state senator and representative if you want them to pass a law to ban cockfighting.

■ You can design posters and t-shirts that say things like "It's not right to make dogs fight." To design a t-shirt, get some inexpensive white t-shirts at a department store and some fabric paint or markers at an art supply or craft store. Draw and paint whatever you want. It's lots of fun. Then wear the t-shirts. You'll be teaching people wherever you go!

Chapter 2. Tricks for Kicks

No One Is Born Vicious

(You'll need a few friends for this game.)

Choose one person to be the trainer. The trainer should yell at the rest of you and be really mean and nasty to get you to do something (without touching or hurting anyone!). After five minutes everyone should tell the trainer how they feel, what their mood is like, what they feel like doing. Next the trainer should be really nice and encouraging and say kind things to get you to do something. After five minutes, everyone should tell the trainer how they feel again. What did you find out? How does mean training make you feel? How does nice training make you feel? Do you understand how a dog could be made to be vicious by a cruel trainer?

People use the word "chicken" to describe a coward. In fact, chickens are quite brave. That's one of the reasons why they're used in cockfights!

chapter

3

Furry, Fuzzy and Feathery

Animals Whom People Wear

Did you know that you probably wear parts of animals all the time? Maybe you don't believe me, but go open your closet and check for yourself. Do you have leather shoes or a leather belt or even a little bit of leather on your sneakers? Do you have a wool coat or sweater or hat or scarf? Do you have any pearls or coral? Do you have sheepskin slippers or fur muffs? Do you carry a rabbit's foot? It's important to know these things because once you know you can make choices to help save animals. If you want to help the animals people wear, just turn the page ...

... and then go save some lives!

Cast Your Votes About Fur Coats

When I was a kid I used to love touching my mother's fur coat. The fur was soft and shiny, and I liked running my fingers through it. I didn't think a lot about where the fur had come from. I just assumed that when animals died of old age, people took their fur and made coats out of it. I was very wrong about that.

Some wild animals are raised on fur "ranches" just so that people can kill them and cut off their fur and skin to make coats. Animals in fur "ranches" spend their whole lives in small, cramped, wire cages.

Other animals who are killed for their fur are trapped in the wild. One kind of trap, called a steel-jaw leghold trap, works like this: an animal, such as a raccoon, smells food and goes over to investigate. The raccoon doesn't know that some person put the food out to trap her. She walks over to the food, but she doesn't see the trap. Suddenly, she steps on a steel plate. Before she has time to figure out what's going on, metal jaws spring shut around her leg. She cries out because her leg hurts so much, but there's nothing her family can do to save her. She tries to get out of the trap, but she can't move. Eventually, the trapper comes and kills her (if she hasn't already bled or starved to death).

Get Some Facts!

■ Most of the animals who are raised on fur ranches are wild animals such as minks and foxes. It's very unnatural for them to be in tiny, open cages. They can't dig holes in the ground or get away from people or noise.

■ Animals sometimes remain in traps for a long time before the trapper comes to kill them. While they're in the traps they can't get any food or water; they can't hide, and they can't get out of the rain or snow, either.

■ Some animals will actually chew off their own foot to escape the trap!

■ Even though trappers only want to catch certain kinds of animals, like foxes, raccoons, and beavers, other animals, such as dogs, cats and eagles, get caught, too. Trappers call these animals "trash animals" because the traps were not intended for them. If you live near woods where people trap animals and you let your dog and cat run around alone, they could get caught in a trap!

Some Things You Can Do to Save Furry Animals

■ You can avoid fur. You might not think you would ever buy fur, but fur sneaks into clothes when you don't expect to see it. For example, gloves are sometimes lined with fur, and jackets are sometimes trimmed with it. You might find fur on a hat or on ear muffs. Keep your eyes open, and let your family know if you don't want any presents which have fur in them.

■ If you get something with fur in it as a gift, you can still say "thank you." You might want to very politely tell the person how you feel about fur though so they know not to buy it for you any more. If you're nice about it, they'll probably be very understanding, and they'll learn about fur just like you have.

■ You can stop into fancy toy stores and look for stuffed animals and holiday nutcrackers with real fur on them. If you write to the manager of the store to say how you feel about fur toys, he or she may decide not to sell real fur any more.

■ Ask your parents if you can put a bumper sticker on the car about fur coats. You can get bumper stickers from Friends of Animals (P.O. Box 1244, Norwalk, CT 06856) or PETA (P.O. Box 42516, Washington, DC 20015).

It takes 40 raccoons to make one raccoon fur coat and up to 200 chinchillas to make one chinchilla fur coat. Chinchilla hairs are so fine that it takes 60 of them to equal the thickness of a human hair.

■ Lots of people in the Congress of the United States are trying to make the leghold traps illegal. You can write to your senators and representative and ask them to vote against cruel traps. Ask your parents the names of your senators and representative in Congress. Here are their addresses:

Senators

(Name of Senator)
United States Senate
Washington, DC
20510

Representatives

(Name of Representative)
House of Representatives
Washington, DC
20515

The proper way to address your letters is: The Honorable _____. So if your senator is named Lucy Laws, you would address your letter to The Honorable Lucy Laws.

■ When Congress is about to vote about a law you can write a letter to the editor of your local newspaper to let other people know that they can contact their senators and representative and express their opinions, too.

■ There are groups which will send you more information and give you other ideas about helping furry animals. Their names and numbers are listed in the "To Learn More" section, at the end of the book.

Kid Hero

When Hope was ten years old she used to leave messages on her answering machine telling callers how cruel fur is, as well as suggestions for helping animals. Every time someone called her up, they'd hear a new message about how to save animals.

Who's Wary of Wool?

Wool is sheep fur, but it's different from mink fur or fox fur because you don't have to kill the sheep to get it, which is good. What's not so good is that some people are pretty mean to the sheep they raise for wool.

If you lived with a sheep who got really woolly, and in the springtime you gave her a haircut and then used her wool to make a sweater or coat or rug, you probably wouldn't hurt her. Unfortunately, that's not how most people get their wool. Most wool comes from sheep who live on big, crowded farms in Australia.

Sheep's wool can get pretty dirty and sometimes bugs get into it, especially the wool around their rear ends. On a lot of the big sheep farms in Australia, people cut off the skin around the sheep's rear ends so that the wool won't grow there anymore. It's called mulesing. Can you imagine if someone cut off your skin? OUCH!

Chapter 3. Furry, Fuzzy and Feathery

Get Some Facts!

- Sheep from Australia are often sent to other countries on crowded ships. The sheep are treated so badly on the ships that a lot of them die.

- Some sheep have their fur cut off when it's still cold out. It takes awhile before their fur grows back. They can get very cold without their wool coats.

- Wool coats and sweaters in stores usually came from the sheep in Australia.

- Lots of people aren't careful when they shear sheep, and they handle the sheep roughly or cut them when shaving.

Some Things You Can Do to Help Sheep

Big Horn sheep have been described as having vision similar to a human who is using binoculars!

- If you decide that you'd rather not wear wool, you can ask your parents and grandparents to buy you clothes made from cotton, flannel, corduroy and other materials. If you do get a wool sweater for your birthday, remember that not everyone knows what happens to sheep. You can let your family know, which is a great way to help animals.

- Read labels on clothes and learn what the words mean by looking them up in a dictionary. Once you know, you can be careful when you and your parents go shopping.

- Look for fun clothes in thrift shops. You'll know that no new animals were hurt, and you may find some really cool things for only a few cents or dollars!

What's Down with Down?

The soft feathers of geese and ducks are called down. Down is warm and light, and people like to use it to stuff pillows, jackets, comforters and sleeping bags. If you're like me when I was a kid, you might think that it's only when geese and ducks die of old age that people take their feathers. Too bad that's not how it works. Most of the time people kill ducks and geese and then use their feathers.

Get Some Facts!

■ Most ducks and geese are raised on crowded farms where they can't fly or find a spot to be alone or stretch their wings.

■ Some down is pulled right out of geese while they're still alive. Pulling out feathers on a bird is like pulling out hair on a person. Imagine if someone grabbed handfuls of your hair and yanked it out!

Some Things You Can Do to Help Ducks and Geese

■ If you need a sleeping bag or a winter jacket, you can ask your parents to choose one stuffed with fiberfill or some other warm, synthetic material that isn't from animals.

■ If you already have feather pillows and comforters at home, make sure they last a long time so you don't need any new pillows or comforters.

■ Enjoy making a feather garden from feathers which fell off birds freely.

You'll need:

☞ a pretty bowl

☞ enough sand or dirt to fill the bowl

☞ feathers which you find in the woods

☞ a piece of paper and a pen

Fill the bowl with the sand or dirt and then stick the feathers in the bowl. Arrange them however you think they look best. On the piece of paper you can write in your neatest handwriting: THESE FEATHERS FELL FREELY; LET BIRDS LIVE! and place the sign above or in front of your feather garden. Whenever someone asks you about your feather garden, you can also tell them about down.

Feathers help keep ducks and geese from getting wet. Even though these birds swim and dive, they don't get wet because the water just rolls off their feathers.

Considering Whether to Wear Leather

Did you ever wonder where leather comes from? Leather is the skin of animals, usually cows, pigs and sheep. I'll be telling you about what life is like for these animals in the section called "Meet Your Meat." I'll let you know right now that life can be pretty awful for most cows and pigs and a lot of sheep. That's why some people who want to help these animals don't wear their skin.

Get Some Facts!

■ Lots of things may be made out of leather including jackets, pocketbooks, shoes, belts, wallets, watchbands, chairs, couches and much more.

■ In order to turn cow skin or pig skin into leather, people have to clean it and put chemicals on it. This process is called tanning, and tanning can cause a lot of pollution.

■ Many people wear animal skin in order to feel fashionable. For example, people walk around in alligator and snake skin shoes and carry eel skin wallets. Some people wear leather jackets which they think are very fashionable.

Some Things You Can Do to Help Pigs, Cows and Sheep

■ If you want, you can let your family know you'd rather have rubber or canvas shoes than leather shoes. If they want to get you leather shoes really badly, then make sure you take good care of them, so you won't need another pair too soon.

■ Leather jackets aren't really cool when you think about the fact that leather hurts animals and the environment. You might prefer to wear a really cool, flannel-lined, pre-washed jeans jacket than a dead cow skin.

■ Go animal sleuthing in malls and department stores by looking for animal skins. If you see animal skins, you can write to the manager of the store and ask if the store might be willing to sell the same kinds of items made with cotton or synthetic fabric.

■ You can always choose a canvas watchband, or a cloth book bag or a nylon wallet. They're less expensive than leather, too!

Leather has a very distinctive smell. You can usually tell if something is made out of leather by smelling it.

Boycotting Beastly Beads and Baubles

Dead animal parts show up everywhere. There are beads made out of sea creatures, sculptures made out of elephant tusks, and earrings made from animal bones or horns. Jewelry and sculptures are nice, but I think it's pretty silly to kill animals just for a necklace or bracelet.

Get Some Facts!

- Pearls are beads which grow inside oysters.

- When an elephant tusk is carved into jewelry or a sculpture it's called ivory.

- Elephants are killed just so that people can have ivory, and rhinos are killed just for their horns.

- Elephants and walruses are endangered. That means there aren't too many left in the world. One of the reasons why they're endangered is that people are killing them for their white tusks.

- One of the reasons why coral reefs are disappearing is because people are killing all the coral for jewelry and fish tanks.

Some Things You Can Do to Help

- You can avoid coral, pearls, ivory, tortoise shell, bone or horn jewelry, and you can also teach your parents and friends about jewelry from animals.

- You can write your senators and representative asking them to ban ivory from entering the United States. If every country banned ivory, then people wouldn't kill the elephants!

■ You can make your own jewelry. Here's how:

You'll need:

☞ clay (Some craft stores sell special clay for molding jewelry.)

☞ a toothpick

☞ ceramic paint

☞ string

1.

Mold the clay into small balls and use the toothpick to make holes through the center.

2.

Let the clay dry thoroughly.

3.

After the clay balls are dry, paint them however you like.

4.

If you have a kiln at school, ask your teacher to fire the clay balls. They'll last longer that way.

5.

Thread the clay beads onto the string. Presto, you have a necklace or bracelet!

People have observed wild elephants crying out when their young have died and covering the dead elephants with dirt, grass and leaves.

Are Animals' Heads Dead?
Do Animals' Tails Fail?

You just learned how dead animal parts show up in jewelry, but have you noticed that dead animals pop up in other places, too? Some stores sell raccoon, fox or squirrel tails for people to hang from a hat or in their car or some other place. You might see a rabbit's foot sold on a key chain, or a deer's whole head sold to people to hang on a wall.

I think it's pretty gross to hang parts of animals on the wall or from key chains. Imagine if people's heads were mounted above the fireplace, or people's fingers were attached to key chains. Yuck!

Get Some Facts!

■ Animal parts which are sold for decoration don't come from animals who have died naturally. They come from animals who were killed by people.

■ Some people think that having a rabbit's foot brings luck. That's not true. Having a rabbit's foot just means that some poor rabbit was unlucky.

■ Stuffing dead animals for display is called taxidermy. Taxidermists use poisonous chemicals when they stuff dead animals. Be careful not to touch a stuffed dead animal.

■ There's a beautiful monkey who lives in Africa called a Colobus. Colobus monkeys have long, thick, black and white tails. Some people kill these monkeys just to use their tails for small, throw rugs, and it takes 25 or more tails to make one rug!

Chapter 3. Furry, Fuzzy and Feathery

Some Things You Can Do to Help

■ If you don't want to contribute to the death of animals for trinkets, be careful that you don't accidentally buy a part of a dead animal. Sometimes they turn up where you don't expect them. For example, a lot of hats have feathers in them. Feathers do fall freely from birds, but very few people go into the woods to look for fallen feathers. The feathers in feather dusters or on hats practically always come from birds who were killed by people.

Birds molt their feathers. That means that they shed them, just like mammals shed their fur. New feathers grow to replace the old ones.

■ Go animal sleuthing: you can visit stores in a mall or shopping center and check for dead animal parts. If you see any, you can write to the store manager about how it makes you feel to see animal parts for sale!

■ Make your own decorations! Here's how to make an animal floor mat:

You'll need:

☞ a big piece of thick canvas
☞ paint and brushes

Draw a design of an animal on the canvas and then paint it in. Let it dry. Presto, you've got a floor mat or a wall hanging!

chapter

4

Meet Your Meat

Animals Whom People Eat

I used to know a black sheep who always ran up to greet me when I visited him. He'd tilt his head back so that I could pet him under his chin. I named him Woolly Baba, and he was one of my friends when I was a kid.

One day when I was eating my favorite dinner, which was lamb chops, I started thinking about Woolly Baba. All of a sudden I got this very funny feeling in my stomach. Even though my food didn't look at all like Woolly Baba, I knew that the lamb chop I was eating was once a part of a sheep just like my friend.

Then I started to realize that my hamburger was cow flesh, and my ham sandwich was pig flesh, and my chicken dinner was once a chicken and my tuna salad was a fish. It may seem funny to you that I didn't know that the chicken I ate was once a living, breathing, clucking chicken, but I really hadn't realized that I was eating my friends.

More animals are killed for food than for any other reason. In fact, more animals are killed every year in the United States for food than there are people in the whole world! In this section, I'll be telling you about animals we eat. There's a lot that you can do to help these animals, so just turn the page ...

... and then go save some lives!

Behind the Barnyard

Meat is a funny word because it doesn't really tell you much about your food. We use a lot of words for food which don't tell us much. For example, what does a hamburger animal look like? or a hot dog animal? or a steak or bacon animal?

Hamburger is really ground up cow, and bacon is really strips of pig flesh, and a hot dog is really a mishmash of dead animal parts. When you talk about food that way, it certainly sounds different, doesn't it?

Hundreds of millions of cows, pigs and sheep are killed every year for hamburgers, hot dogs, bacon and lamb chops. A lot of them have really awful lives before they're killed, too. Hardly any pigs get to swim in shallow ponds, or stretch out with other pigs in the dirt anymore. Most pigs live in tiny compartments in smelly buildings where they can't move around much or play in the sunshine. Most mother pigs have the worst life of all. They live in cramped, narrow stalls practically their whole lives! The buildings are so filthy that the pigs often get very sick.

You probably think that cattle spend their whole lives grazing on grass on wide open fields. Part of their lives, maybe, but not all. Most cattle are shipped to crowded, dusty feedlots, which are kind of like parking lots for animals, where they are fattened before they are killed.

Get Some Facts about Pigs and Cows!

- If someone tells you that pigs are dirty, you can give them the real facts. Pigs like to stay clean, but if they're outside in the sun they can get sunburned and hot just like people, so they'll roll in the mud to protect themselves and stay cool. That's pretty smart!

- Most animals raised and killed for food no longer live out their lives in open barns or in spacious, outdoor enclosures. Most spend their lives in closed, smelly buildings which look more like factories than farms. People call these "modern" agriculture units "factory farms."

- The hard floors which most pigs live on in factory farms are very bad for their feet. Their legs can get injured and deformed which causes them a lot of pain.

■ When cows and pigs are taken to slaughterhouses (that's where they're killed) they're often forced onto crowded trucks with an electric prod. An electric prod is a big stick which has an electric charge stored in it. If someone used an electric prod on you, it would feel like the worst, most painful shock you can imagine!

■ People burn marks on cows with a hot iron so they can tell the cows apart. It's called branding. They rarely give the cows anything to stop the pain. Imagine if someone burned a big mark on your skin with an iron.

■ To mark pigs, some people cut off pieces of their ears!

■ Many pigs go crazy inside the crowded buildings and cages just like dogs would go crazy if you put them in stinky, dirty places with hundreds of other dogs. When the pigs go crazy they sometimes start to bite each other's tails. To keep this from happening, people cut off their tails without giving them any pain killers!

Get Some Facts about Eating Animals!

■ People who don't eat animals are called vegetarians.

■ One out of every two men who eats animals regularly will get a heart attack.

- Only one out of every twenty men who are strict vegetarians will get a heart attack. A strict vegetarian, called a vegan (pronounced vee-gan), doesn't eat any animals or animal products, including eggs, foods made out of milk (such as cheese or yogurt), and sometimes honey.

- People who eat animals are more likely to get certain kinds of cancer than vegetarians.

- Almost all of the corn, oats and soybeans grown in America are fed to animals.

- If we grew corn, oats and soybeans to feed to people instead of to animals, we would have enough food to feed all the starving people in the world.

- Pigs and cows produce a lot of waste that pollutes the earth.

- Cows, pigs and other animals whom people eat use up more water than all the people in the United States use for all purposes including drinking, washing, watering gardens and filling swimming pools.

- On average, vegetarians live several years longer than people who eat animals.

- Vegetarians get the vitamins, protein and minerals that they need from plants.

- As long as there are grains, nuts, fruits, beans and vegetables around, nobody needs to eat animals!

Some Things You Can Do to Save Pigs, Cows and Sheep

■ Probably the best way you can help cows, pigs and sheep is not to eat them. If you think that it would be hard to give up hot dogs, hamburgers, spareribs, lamb chops and sausage, you might try eating fewer animals. That will help cows, pigs and sheep a lot! If your parents want you to eat animals, share your feelings with them and get some books on vegetarian nutrition which you can read together. You may have to compromise, which is okay. See page 189 for names of cookbooks and other good books to read.

■ Try eating soy dogs, bean burgers, spaghetti with meatless tomato sauce, bean tacos and burritos, peanut butter and jelly sandwiches (or peanut butter and banana sandwiches), stir-fried vegetables, vegetarian chili and other yummy vegetarian foods. Ask your parents to help you find the ingredients and prepare these delicious foods with them.

Chapter 4. Meet Your Meat

- Maybe your parents would be willing to have a vegetarian dinner a couple of nights a week for your family's health, for the environment and for the animals.

- Visit a health food store and try out some of the different vegetarian foods.

- If your family goes out to restaurants, ask if you can try Indian, Chinese, Mexican or Italian restaurants where there are lots of vegetarian dishes.

- You, your friends and your parents can ask your school to serve good vegetarian lunches.

- Find a friend who also cares about animals. You can try out vegetarian foods together!

- If you don't eat animals, you can wear a button or a t-shirt which says "I'm a vegetarian - I don't eat my friends!"

- Go animal sleuthing in the supermarket. Look for foods which have animals in them. Sometimes animal foods are obvious, like in the meat section. Other times, animal foods such as lard or animal oils are hidden in foods like cookies and cakes.

Pigs are very intelligent. Some people think that they're smarter than dogs!

- Trace a package of bacon from the supermarket to the pig who was killed for it. Ask the butcher or the manager where the bacon came from. Try doing some serious detective work with your family by visiting the place where the pigs are raised for ham and bacon.

Making up Animal Compliments

(You can do this game alone, but it's more fun with a friend.)

Write down a list of all the insults people say which use animals (like "you're a pig" or "what a bully"). Make up some compliments using animals (like "she's patient as a cow" or "he's as playful as a pig taking a bath"). Try using the compliments. You'll change people's thinking about animals!

Veggie Talk

(You'll need a friend for this role play.)

Choose one person to be a vegetarian and the other to tease the vegetarian for not eating animals. The vegetarian should practice responding calmly and teaching the teaser about animal cruelty. The vegetarian might try to encourage the teaser to avoid eating animals, too! Switch roles and keep practicing until you feel confident. Tell each other which answers worked best.

Kid Hero

When Jenifer Graham of California was 11 years old she used to sneak off when she and her mom went to the supermarket. While her mom was busy shopping, Jenifer was busy putting stickers on the meat products. The stickers said: "Animals suffered to make this product - Don't eat meat!" When Jenifer got older she refused to cut up a frog in science class. She went to court to fight for her right to refuse, and guess what happened? California passed a law which gives students the right not to cut up animals in school!

Meals of Veal

Have you ever had veal cutlets or veal scaloppini? Did you wonder what veal really was? Well, veal is the flesh of a baby cow, called a calf. It makes me sad to tell you about veal calves, but the best way to help the calves is to let you know what's going on so that you can decide for yourself whether to have a meal of veal.

Some people like to drink the milk from cows. In order for a dairy cow to produce milk she has to keep having babies. When the cows have female calves, they're likely to grow up to be dairy cows like their mom. When the cows have male calves, though, many of them are taken away from their moms to be raised for veal.

Some of the veal calves are taken away from their moms only a few hours to a day or two after they're born, and they're put in tiny, wooden stalls all by themselves. They're chained at the neck so they can't turn around or move more than a step backward or forward. All they can do is stand up or lie down. Twice a day, for about twenty minutes, they're given some liquid, milk food. Other than that, nothing happens at all. They never get to play, or graze on the grass, or feel the sunshine on their backs, or be with their mothers. The calves spend their whole lives in the little stalls until they're big enough to be killed and turned into veal.

The reason why the calves are chained is so they won't move around and develop muscles. You know how muscles work, right? The more you use them, the bigger they get. People who raise veal calves don't want them to have strong muscles because muscles make the veal tougher, and veal is known for being very tender.

Get Some Facts!

■ One million calves are raised and killed for veal every year in the United States.

■ In addition to being tender, veal is also known for being very light-colored. The reason why the veal is whitish is because the calves weren't given very much iron in their food. Iron would make their flesh pink. Calves need iron in their diet just like people. Even though they're given some iron, it's not as much as they should get.

- The calves raised like this can get sick easily. In order to keep them alive, they're usually fed drugs.

- When the calves are big enough, they're forced to walk to the trucks which will take them to the slaughterhouse to be killed. The calves haven't walked since they were a couple of days old so their muscles are very weak. In order to make them walk, some people use electric prods on them.

- The calves are never given solid food to eat, so they often have diarrhea.

- Since cows have to keep having babies in order to produce milk, we have lots of veal calves. If people didn't drink cow's milk, we'd have less veal.

- Most of the cows who give us milk are hooked to milking machines in big buildings every day. Their udders are so huge, and they are forced to make so much milk that most of them get an udder infection called mastitis. Mastitis is very painful.

Some Things You Can Do to Save Veal Calves

- Of course, the best way to help veal calves is to not eat veal. You can also tell everybody you know about what happens to baby cows for veal.

- Become an artist for animals! If you decide not to eat veal, you can paint a t-shirt that says "I don't eat meals of veal" and wear it when you go out. When people ask why not, you can teach them about veal calves.

■ You may want to check the menus at nearby restaurants. If you see a menu with veal on it, you can write or talk to the manager and explain about veal calves.

■ The reason we have so many veal calves is because we keep making cows give us milk. You can help veal calves by drinking less milk and eating less cheese and ice cream. You can substitute soy milk for cow's milk. Soy milk is actually made from soy beans and comes in different flavors. You can visit your local health food store for ice cream and cheese substitutes, too. You can even have Pizzsoy, which is pizza with soy cheese.

■ You can write to your senators and representative in Congress about passing a law to provide a better life for veal calves.

■ You can contact some of the groups listed in the back of the book if you want to learn more about animals who are raised for food. Some organizations, like Farm Sanctuary, have programs in which you can adopt rescued animals!

Within hours of birth, calves can walk!

Chapter 4. Meet Your Meat

Life as a Veal Calf

You'll need:

- ☞ a big cardboard box, like the kind refrigerators come in
- ☞ a felt tip marker
- ☞ big scissors
- ☞ a parent to help you
- ☞ friends to share the experience with you

1.

Draw bars on each side of the cardboard box.

2.

Have your parent cut out the box around the bars so the box looks like a crate or jail.

3.

Have your parent lift the box over your head so you're standing inside it.

4.

Have them leave you in your room with the lights dimmed. Ask your friends to be very quiet in the room with you.

5.

Stay in the box for awhile.

6.

When you feel ready, get out.

7.

Write down how you felt, and what you think it would be like to spend your whole life in a box like that, only getting food twice a day. Now you have some idea of what it must be like for veal calves.

8.

Take turns, and let your friends try it, too.

9.

Share your experiences with each other, and describe your feelings.

Who Came First, the Chicken or the Egg?

Close your eyes and imagine a chicken or a turkey on a farm. What does the farm look like? What is the bird doing? Now that you have a clear picture in your mind, I'm going to tell you what life is really like for practically all chickens and turkeys in the United States.

Some people eat both the flesh of chickens and turkeys as well as the eggs of hens. These days, people eat so many eggs and so many chickens that billions of chickens are killed every year, and hundreds of millions are forced to spend their lives laying eggs all the time in factory farms. This is how it works: chickens and turkeys who are raised for their flesh are put in big buildings where they're crowded together with so many other birds that they can hardly move. They spend their whole

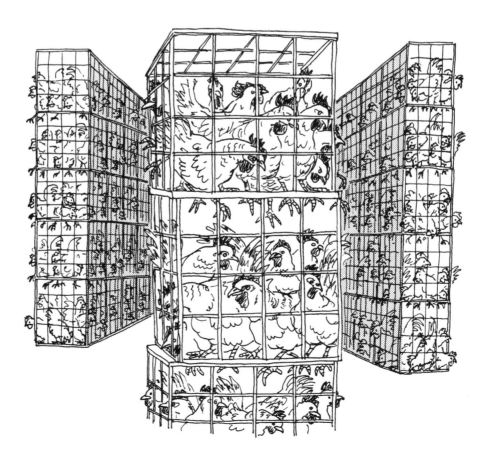

lives like this until they're fat enough to be killed for food. Then they're stuffed into little crates, and the crates are piled up onto trucks which take them to slaughterhouses to be killed. When they get to the slaughterhouses, the birds are hung upside down by their feet on a conveyor belt (that's a machine which carries the birds from one place to another). The birds are aware of everything that happens to them until they're stunned or killed.

For the hens who lay eggs, life is even worse. Almost all the hens are stuffed into cages so tightly that there's no room to even stretch their wings! The cages are stacked on top of each other in huge factory farm buildings. Hundreds of thousands of chickens live in just one building. The buildings smell so bad that you could barely breathe inside of them, but the chickens have to breathe inside them for their whole lives. Lots of the chickens die in their cages because they can't get to their food, or because other chickens trample them since there's so little room, or because they get sick. Remember how the veal calves are fed drugs to keep them alive? Well, so are the chickens, but the cages are so dirty and crowded that even the drugs can't keep them all alive.

Chickens and turkeys are birds just like parakeets, robins, pheasants and canaries. Maybe they're not as pretty as these other birds, but they have similar feelings. Can you imagine treating pet birds and wild birds the way the chickens and turkeys are treated?

Get Some Facts!

■ It's against the law to put canaries or parrots in cages like the ones the chickens are kept in, but no laws protect the chickens and turkeys.

■ Male chickens don't lay eggs, so when chicks are born for egg-laying, the male chicks are often thrown into a garbage can - while they're still alive!

■ Chickens need room to move around, just like people. When chickens are put into crowded cages, they go crazy and start to peck each other to death. To keep the chickens from killing each other, their sharp beaks are cut off with a hot blade when they're very young. No pain killers are given to the chicks at all!

■ Because of the way the chickens are raised, a lot of them carry diseases that can make people very sick if they're not careful when they cook chickens.

■ Turkeys are bred to be big and fat so that there will be a lot of flesh on them. That's not too good for the turkeys. Sometimes they're so fat they can barely walk.

■ When chickens spend their whole lives in cages, their toe-nails don't get worn down. Their nails sometimes grow so long they curl around the wires of the cages and back into the chickens' feet. When that happens the chickens can't get to their food and water, and so they die. To keep this from happening, some people cut off the chickens' toes, not just their toenails!

■ Eggs have lots of fat and cholesterol in them. Too much fat and cholesterol makes people sick!

Some Things You Can Do to Save Chickens and Turkeys

■ The best thing you can do for chickens and turkeys is not to eat them or their eggs, but if you don't think that you're ready to give them up, then ask your parents if you can get them from health food stores and nearby farms where the chickens and turkeys aren't raised in cages. There are still some farmers (but not many) who raise chickens and turkeys outside on real farms.

■ Avoid buying white eggs from the supermarket. If you choose to eat eggs, you can get brown eggs from nearby farmers and health food stores. Eggs from chickens who roam around barnyards and live normal, healthy lives are called "fertile eggs" or "free-roaming chicken eggs." Some of these eggs come from chickens who weren't treated much better than the caged hens, though, so you may want to check out the farm with your parents.

■ Be an animal advertisement sleuth. Go to the supermarket and look at the egg cartons and chicken packaging. Are there any drawings or pictures of chickens? Are the chickens in small, dirty cages? Are they missing half of their beaks? Or do they look like the chickens you imagined when you first started reading this chapter? You can draw pictures and make posters showing what it's really like for chickens. Hang the pictures and posters up at school, in church, at the YWCA or YMHA, in synagogues, in libraries and wherever else you can. You can let people know all about what happens to chickens!

- If you see an advertisement for chickens or eggs on TV which tells people that the chickens live happy lives, you can write to the TV station and ask the producer to stop showing advertisements which are not true.

- If you like writing these letters, you can also write to your local newspapers and ask them to publish an article about chickens and how they are raised.

- Go animal sleuthing: ask the manager at the supermarket where their eggs come from and then go with your parents to see for yourself how the chickens are raised for food.

- If you want more information about helping chickens you can contact United Poultry Concerns. Their address and phone number is in the section "To Learn More," at the end of the book.

Life as an Egg-laying Hen

You'll need:
- ☞ a small closet
- ☞ five friends
- ☞ an adult to supervise this experiment

An adult must supervise this experiment. Climb into the small closet with your friends making sure that you don't lock the door. You should be so crowded that you can barely turn around. Stay there for fifteen minutes (unless you can't stand it, and you feel like you have to get out). After you get out of the closet talk about how it felt to be crowded together. How would it feel to spend your whole life in there? Is that what life is like for an egg-laying hen? Remember: you could leave the closet if you wanted to, but the chickens can't ever leave their cages.

Chapter 4. Meet Your Meat

Riddle

Question: Why did the chicken cross the road?

Answer: To be with the vegetarians!

Kid Hero

When Matthew went off to summer camp, he brought along lots of pamphlets and flyers about saving animals. There were so many campers and counselors interested in learning how to save animals that the camp gave Matthew his own office where he could hand out information. Matthew encouraged other campers to help him save animals by becoming vegetarians. Soon the camp was serving vegetarian meals for everybody.

Here's another fact about the bravery of chickens: mother chickens will fight off crows and other animals who try to attack their chicks.

Duck a Goose

Have you ever fed the ducks and geese at a nearby pond or lake? It's fun to feed the birds and to listen to them quack and honk, and to watch them swim and float and fly. Some people like to eat ducks and parts of geese. There's a very expensive food called goose-liver paté. In order to make this food, people put tubes down the throat of a goose while she's awake and aware of everything that's happening to her, and then they force food into her through the tube. They give her so much food that she gets sick. That makes her liver swell up, and once her liver is all big and swollen, she's killed, and her liver is removed. Then people use her liver to make the paté.

Get Some Facts!

■ People don't need to eat ducks or geese (or chickens, cows, or pigs either!).

■ Geese get married. They don't have a special ceremony like people do, but once a goose finds a mate, the two spend their whole lives together.

■ Ducks and geese are very good mothers. They keep their ducklings and goslings (that's the name for baby geese) close by, and they chase anyone who gets too close.

Some Things You Can Do to Help Ducks and Geese

■ You can avoid goose-liver paté, and tell your friends and your family about how the paté is made.

■ Consider whether you want to eat ducks, and if you don't want to eat them, talk to your parents about how it makes you feel to think about having ducks for dinner.

■ You can feed the ducks and geese at ponds and lakes, but don't feed them bread. Bread can make them sick when it expands in their bodies. Get cracked corn instead. Yum, yum, yum.

Ducks and geese can fly, float, walk and swim. There aren't too many animals who can do all that!

Go Fish?

I've already talked to you about fishes. You've learned that it's painful for fishes to be hooked, and that fishes can't breathe when they're out of the water. Getting caught by a hook or in a big net isn't too much fun for fishes, but a lot of people like to eat them, so they catch fishes anyway. Other sea creatures like lobsters, crabs and shrimp are caught and killed for food, too.

**Lobsters live a long time.
Some live almost 100 years!**

Get Some Facts!

■ People have killed so many fishes that some kinds of fish are almost all gone.

■ A lot of the pollution and poisons people put in the water get eaten by fishes. Some people think fish is a health food, but lots of fishes have very unhealthy poisons in them.

■ Sometimes fishing lines and hooks get lost or left on the beach. The hooks can hurt other animals, and the lines can get tangled around birds and sea creatures.

■ Some stores put live lobsters on ice, or crowd them into little tanks and don't give them any food at all.

■ The most common way to cook lobsters and crabs is to drop them into boiling water while they're still alive.

Some Things You Can Do to Save Fishes

■ You can think about whether or not you really want to eat fishes, lobsters, crabs and shrimp. If you don't want to eat them, talk to your family about your feelings.

■ If you see lobsters crowded into a tank at the supermarket or at a restaurant, you can write to the owner and let her or him know how you feel. Some people have even asked the owners to put the lobsters back in the ocean and stop selling them at the supermarket.

chapter

5

Monkey Business

Animals in Laboratories

Have you ever been inside a laboratory? A lot of them are pretty cool, with lots of machines and computers and amazing experiments going on. Unfortunately, though, some scientists in laboratories experiment on animals, by cutting them up, or giving them poisons, or making them really sick, or testing products on them, or even burning them. And some of the experiments aren't ever going to help anyone! Some people think that it's okay to hurt and kill a few animals if that will help a lot of people. Maybe you think so, too. But guess what? Millions of animals are hurt and killed in laboratories in experiments that never help people. If you want to help those animals, just turn the page ...

... and then go save some lives!

Buying Cruelty-free

Lots of products, like shampoo, soap, toothpaste, bubble bath, suntan lotion, ammonia and even some toys, are tested on animals. That doesn't mean that scientists shampoo rabbits' fur, or brush rats' teeth, or let guinea pigs play with toys. What testing means is that products like shampoo or ammonia are force-fed to animals and dripped into their eyes and rubbed onto their skin. These tests are supposed to show whether or not the products are safe for people to use.

Some of the tests are very cruel. Putting ammonia into a rabbit's eye burns the rabbit's eye a lot. And the rabbits aren't given pain killers.

Lots of products are force-fed to animals until they die. It usually takes a long time for them to die, too, which is really awful.

The ironic thing is that these tests really don't help people. In fact, they don't even keep dangerous products out of stores! For example, ammonia has been tested on rabbits' eyes and has been force-fed to animals and poured on their backs. Animals have even been made to breathe ammonia fumes. Companies found out that ammonia can hurt and kill animals very easily, but that didn't stop them from selling it. Anyone can go to a store and buy as much ammonia as he wants.

There are a lot of companies which don't test their products on animals. They do safety tests in test tubes with living cells and by using computers, and they find out whether a product is safe the modern way.

Get Some Facts!

■ Rabbit eyes and human eyes are very different. Products which hurt rabbits' eyes may not hurt human eyes. Then again, products which don't hurt rabbits' eyes may hurt human eyes.

■ Some products have been force-fed to rats and mice and have had very different effects on each. If there are big differences between rats and mice, imagine how big the differences can be between rats and humans!

■ Animals who are used to test products are rarely, if ever, given any medicine to ease their pain.

■ When the tests on animals are over, the animals are always killed.

■ Testing products on animals is not necessary to protect people. There are all sorts of tests which don't use animals that companies can use to find out whether their products are safe.

■ Hundreds of companies don't test their products on animals, and their products are just as safe.

Some Things You Can Do to Stop Testing on Animals

■ You can go cruelty-free by avoiding products which were tested on animals. Here's how you can make sure that you use cruelty-free products: get a list of companies which do not test their products on animals. (You can call or write PETA, P.O. Box 42516, Washington, DC 20015 (301) 770-7444, and they'll send you a list.) Ask your parents if they'll buy products from the cruelty-free list when they go shopping for shampoo, soap, cosmetics and cleaners. These products can easily be found in health food stores and even in some supermarkets and drug stores.

■ On Halloween, you can dress up like a rabbit or a rat who's been used to test products. When you go trick-or-treating and someone asks you who you are, you can tell them not only who you are, but also about testing products on animals. You can also give them a copy of the list of companies which don't test on animals. Then they can save animals, too!

Wild rabbits in the United States are usually brown so they blend in with the colors in the woods. The rabbits in labs are usually white with pink eyes. The white rabbits are called albinos.

■ You can write to the companies which still test on animals (you can get a list of these companies from PETA, too) and tell them how you feel about their tests. If they tell you they do the tests to protect you, ask them why so many other companies don't test on animals, and no one gets hurt. Are new and improved shampoos, soaps and cosmetics more important than animals' lives? You can let the companies know just how you feel.

■ Go animal sleuthing in drug stores and supermarkets. Take your lists of cruelty-free and cruelty-full companies to the stores and see how many products come from companies which test on animals. You'll need to read the labels closely to find out which companies make the products. You can write to the manager of the store and say how you feel about animal testing. You can even ask the manager to carry more cruelty-free products!

Write it Down

Have a few friends over to your house and spend an hour writing letters to companies which test their products on animals. You can find the addresses of the companies right on the products themselves. You can do this once a month, and really make a difference for animals.

Kid Hero

Nicole, a junior high school student from New Jersey, won first place for her science fair project which showed how cruel and unnecessary animal tests are. Lots of kids saw Nicole's project and learned how to go cruelty-free!

Investigating Animal Experiments

Some animal experiments are done just to test products like shampoo. Others are done to find cures for diseases or to learn about biology or psychology. That doesn't necessarily make them good, though. Lots of experiments are so cruel it's hard to believe that people really do them, or that they're legal.

Here's one:

Animal experimenters took baby monkeys away from their mothers when they were just born. The mothers went crazy worrying about their babies, and their babies were scared, and lonely and went crazy without their mothers. The experimenters put the baby monkeys in small, metal cages all by themselves. Then the experimenters played with the babies with puppets to make the babies think that they were safe and had another mom. But once the babies felt safe with the puppets, the experimenters made the puppets hurt the babies! Some of the puppets were actually machines that shook the baby monkeys really hard, while other puppets had sharp spikes poking out which cut the baby monkeys. Believe it or not, these kinds of experiments still go on today!

Here's another:

Even though we know that smoking cigarettes gives people cancer, some animal experimenters are still making dogs and other animals inhale cigarette smoke. Some experimenters want to prove that smoking doesn't cause cancer in animals. That's silly. Whether or not smoking causes cancer in dogs or other animals, we already know smoking causes cancer in people! What's interesting is that we knew that smoking cigarettes caused lung disease by studying people who smoke. But no warning labels were put on cigarette packages because dogs and other animals didn't get lung disease when they were forced to breathe tobacco smoke. In the case of cigarettes, animal experiments probably caused many people to die by delaying warning labels!

This will be the last one:

Animal experimenters who are working for the Army test deadly weapons on animals while the animals are wide awake! They may detonate explosives on animals, or test chemical weapons on them. In one experiment, cats were shot in the brain. They were asleep while they were shot, but the ones who survived were allowed to wake up in a lot of pain.

You see, not all experiments on animals help people, and some experiments are so cruel that it shouldn't even matter if they help people! Unfortunately, animals in laboratories have hardly any legal protection. In fact, there is no experiment, no matter how painful or useless, which is illegal in the United States.

Get Some Facts!

■ A lot of money is spent to find cures for diseases by making animals sick, but hardly any money is spent to prevent diseases. Remember how you learned that eating a lot of animals can make you ill? Well, instead of teaching people how to eat in a healthy way, we spend most of our money making animals sick to cure the diseases which could be easily prevented by a better diet.

■ Animals don't do drugs, except in laboratories! Animal experimenters are spending millions of dollars making dogs, cats, monkeys and other animals become drug addicts. Meanwhile, human drug addicts can't get into hospitals for treatment because there's not enough money to help them!

■ People will kill a whole family of monkeys in the wild in order to capture one baby monkey for an experiment.

■ Some scientists say that a lot of people would have died because we wouldn't have cures for some diseases without animal experiments, but a lot of people might actually be alive today if we'd spent money teaching people how to take care of themselves and prevent disease instead. Remember what you learned about cancer and heart disease in the chapter "Meet Your Meat?"

■ Some scientists say that people live a lot longer than we used to because of animal experiments, but that's not really true. It is true that people live longer now, but that's not really because of animal experiments! People used to die of diseases because there was no clean water or sanitation. Once people cleaned up their homes and towns and had clean water, they started to live longer. That had nothing to do with hurting and killing animals! Also, most advances in medicine have to do with observing and treating people who are sick, not giving animals diseases. And just because people learned things during animal experiments doesn't mean that that was the only way to learn!

■ When a new medicine is made, all the drug companies want to sell it and make a lot of money. So each company makes its own version of the same medicine, and each company hurts and kills animals to test the same new medicine! If they just shared the results of their tests, or could use alternative, non-animal tests, a lot of animals would be saved.

■ All new drugs are tested on animals before they're tried out on people, but lots of new medicines which seem safe when they're tested on animals turn out to be dangerous to people! That's because all animals are different. For example, aspirin kills cats, and penicillin kills guinea pigs, but both aspirin and penicillin help people.

Some Things You Can Do to Help Animals in Experiments

■ You can write a report on animal experimentation for a school project.

■ You can write your senators and representative to find out if there are any new bills (those are ideas for laws that have to be considered by Congress) about animal experiments. Ask them to send you copies. They'll be hard to read, but you can ask your parents or teachers to help explain them to you. Once you understand them, you can write to your senators and representative to tell them your opinion.

■ If you hear about a particularly cruel and unnecessary experiment (like the ones I told you about in this chapter), you can write to your local newspaper and ask them to do a story about it.

■ You can call up your local animal shelters or SPCA's to find out whether they sell their animals to animal experimenters. Once you know, you can decide whether or not you want to bring any lost or stray animals to them.

■ Interview an animal experimenter. Find out why the experimenter thinks that it's good to experiment on animals. Take notes! Then interview someone who thinks that animal experiments are wrong. You can contact the American Anti-Vivisection Society, 801 Old York Road, #204, Jenkintown, PA 19046 (215) 887-0816 or one of the other groups listed in the "To Learn More" at the end of the book. Think about what you've learned and make your own decision about what you think is right and wrong to do to animals.

Monkeys are a lot like people. They live with their families and friends, they like to play, and they're very protective of those they love.

Electing to Respect

Laboratories aren't just in universities, hospitals and big companies; your school has laboratories, too. They're in the science classrooms (sometimes they're even called science labs!). Every year, millions of frogs are killed and dissected (that means cut apart) in biology classes in schools. Cats, minks, worms, crabs, and pigs are also killed and cut up in biology class.

Kids don't need to dissect animals in order to learn biology, but some schools make students dissect animals anyway. A lot of kids have decided that they won't dissect because they don't believe in killing animals to learn about living creatures.

Your teachers might not ask you to dissect animals right now, but in a few years a science teacher may bring out a dead pig and ask you to cut it up. Remember, you don't have to if you don't want to.

Get Some Facts!

■ Some kinds of frogs are endangered (that means there aren't many left in the wild) because so many are caught and killed. That's not only bad for the frogs, it's also bad for the environment. Frogs eat insects, and in countries where frogs are becoming endangered, there are more and more insects. Some of these insects carry diseases to people or eat crops which people need!

■ Some schools have tried to force students to dissect by threatening them with a bad grade in biology. Some of those students have gone to court to fight for their right not to dissect animals, and guess what? They won!

■ Many of the cats whom people dissect were once someone's companion. Some have come from animal shelters, and some have even been stolen from people's backyards.

■ There are a lot of ways to learn biology without dissecting animals. You can observe live animals in the wild, or you can use plastic models, anatomy books and charts and even computers.

Some Things You Can Do about Dissection in Schools

■ If your teachers want you to dissect or hurt animals, and you don't want to, talk to them and explain that hurting and killing animals is against your beliefs. There are several groups which can help you. They're listed in the "To Learn More" section of this book. You can call one group, the dissection hotline, free: 1-800-922-FROG.

■ If you're a boy or girl scout or you're in the 4-H club and your leaders ask you to hurt an animal, or raise an animal to be killed, you don't have to if you don't want to. No one can make you hurt an animal. If hurting animals upsets you, explain your feelings to them and to your parents.

Every year, millions of animals are killed for school dissections.

■ If your teacher tells the class that it's good or right to use animals in experiments, or for food or sport, you can tell your teacher and your parents that you would like to hear both sides of the story. You can politely ask your teacher to invite someone to speak to the class who thinks that animals shouldn't be hurt in experiments or treated cruelly for food or entertainment. You can even ask the teacher to have a debate with the guest speaker.

Teacher Talk

(You'll need a friend for this role play.)

Choose one person to be the KAAT kid and the other to be the teacher or scout leader. Practice explaining your feelings about hurting animals to the teacher. Switch roles and try again. Discuss which explanations and ways of explaining worked best.

chapter **6**

Buggy, Batty And Badgered

Animals Whom People Don't Like

There are animals whom some people don't like, like cockroaches and mosquitoes and rats and snakes. It's understandable that people might not like animals who bite or hurt them, but just because people don't like some animals doesn't mean we have to hurt or kill them, does it?

If a lion is about to attack you or a mosquito lands on your arm to bite you, and you protect yourself, that makes sense. But if a snake is minding his own business by the side of a trail, and someone hurts that snake, that's just plain mean.

People are messing up the whole planet because we're killing all sorts of animals who really aren't hurting us at all. If you want to help animals, even the ones you might not like too much, then just turn the page ...

... and then go save some lives!

Getting to Know "Pests"

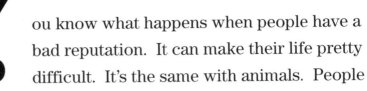

You know what happens when people have a bad reputation. It can make their life pretty difficult. It's the same with animals. People are really mean to animals who have a bad reputation. For example, some people put out poison to kill rats who have a bad reputation. In the West coyotes have a bad reputation, and in the Northeast raccoons have a bad reputation. Snakes have a bad reputation almost everywhere!

Sometimes animals have a bad reputation for a good reason (for instance, they might hurt or kill people), but other times animals have a bad reputation just because they look, smell or act strangely. Even if an animal could hurt someone, that doesn't mean people should be cruel to the animal, does it?

Get Some Facts!

■ Rat poison is very dangerous. Not only does it kill rats slowly and painfully, but any other animals (like dogs or cats) who eat the rats who have died from rat poison may also die. And children who play outside where rat poison has been placed can get very sick.

■ Some mousetraps break the necks of mice and kill them quickly. Other mousetraps - called glue traps - catch mice on a sticky board. The mice may struggle for days and die very slowly because they can't get any food or water. Small companion animals can even get hurt in these traps.

■ Some people kill snakes whenever they see them, but only a few snakes are actually venomous and dangerous to humans. Most snakes are very helpful to farmers, because they eat the mice who like to nibble crops.

Some Things You Can Do for "Pests"

■ Write down a list of animals you don't like. Next to each animal write down whether that animal is really dangerous to you, or whether you don't like the animal for some other reason (such as the animal looks funny or smells bad). Decide whether it's okay to hurt or kill animals who aren't dangerous to you just because you don't like them.

■ Pick an animal you don't like from your list and write a story through that animal's eyes. You might find that you start to care a little bit more about the animal, and once you care, it's easier to be kind.

■ Pick a couple of wild animals you don't like who live near you (they could be moles or bats or armadillos or crows or other animals). If you can, go find these animals in the wild and sit down to observe them. Remember not to disturb the animals! What do they do all day or night? Do they play or make noise? Do they look for food or build houses? After you've spent some time watching the animals, ask yourself if you feel differently about them. Read a book about these animals, too. Once you understand them, you probably won't want to hurt them.

- If you have an unwanted animal "pest" in your home, remove her kindly and cautiously. Don't forget that the animal might be scared and may try to bite. You don't need to use mouse-traps which kill mice. Your family can order a kind mousetrap from Seabright LTD, 4026 Harlan St. Dept. 2, Emeryville, CA 94608, which will catch the mice alive in a little house so that you can let the mouse free outside. You can catch rats in humane traps, too. (Remember: if it's cold outside and the ground is frozen, you can't let a mouse out because he will die if he can't find a warm hole to hide in!)

- There are traps you can use to catch big animals, like raccoons and squirrels, which don't hurt the animals. If you have animals in your attic or chimney, and you want to get them out, you and your family can call the SPCA or shelter and ask where you can borrow a kind trap.

- You can help your parents patch holes in the basement, or build a grate for the chimney, to keep animals from becoming a problem in your house. Keep food and trash tightly sealed, too.

Coyotes are related to dogs. They live in packs and are quite smart.

- Stay away from rat poison! If your family has a problem with rats around the house, keep all food and garbage in tightly sealed containers.

Should We Just Say No to Bug Drugs?

Which animals do you think people like least? I think it's insects. It's true that some insects can be pests, like mosquitoes or fleas or bugs who eat crops, but people haven't thought very carefully about what we should do about insects we don't like. Sometimes people just don't think much at all. Unfortunately, when people don't think carefully, they sometimes do dumb things ...

... like use a lot of insecticides.

Insecticides are very poisonous chemicals which kill insects. People spray insecticides on crops and on gardens to keep insects from eating the fruits and vegetables. But insecticides aren't just dangerous to insects, they can be dangerous to any animals who eat them - including human animals! When people and animals eat the fruits and crops that are sprayed with insecticides, they can get sick. Insecticides also get washed off by rain and get into streams and lakes and the ocean making ocean animals sick and polluting the water.

Not only are insecticides bad for people and animals, they also don't work very well. When people spray insecticides, a few of the insects don't die because the insecticides don't affect them. The surviving insects are resistant to the chemicals. The insects who don't die have babies who aren't affected by the insecticides either, and soon there are a lot of resistant insects. Then the insecticide companies make stronger, more dangerous poisons and spray those on crops. Some of the insects still don't die. Soon, the companies are making really dangerous insecticides. You can see why this is such a big problem.

Get Some Facts!

- Insects play a very important role in a healthy environment!

- Not all insects destroy crops. Some insects eat other insects, but insecticides kill all different kinds of insects, not just the pests.

- Spraying insecticides in your home may not be healthy for you or your companion animals.

- People usually wash fruits and vegetables to get some of the insecticides off, but you can't wash insecticides out of meat and milk. When cows, pigs, sheep, chickens and turkeys are fed foods sprayed with insecticides, they concentrate the insecticides in their own bodies. That means that when people eat meat or drink milk they're often eating more insecticides than if they ate fruits, beans, grains and vegetables.

- Growing crops without insecticides or other poisons is called organic farming. You can learn about organic gardening by reading books from your local library.

You Can Say No to Bug Drugs

■ Ask your parents to help you find organic fruits and vegetables. You can request that your local health food store and even supermarket sell organic food if they don't already.

■ If you want to kill an insect, think hard about whether that insect is going to hurt you or your animals, or whether the insect just looks scary.

■ Fleas can make you and your dog or cat sick, so it makes sense to keep fleas off of your animals. But try not to use insecticides, flea dips or other poisons if you can avoid them! If your cat or dog has fleas, use a flea comb every day. A flea comb is a tiny comb which catches the fleas in its teeth as you comb your animal. You can get one from your vet or at a pet supply store. In order to keep your house flea-free, you'll also need to clean and vacuum rugs and furniture often. You can use herbal collars and sprays and even feed your animals garlic and brewer's yeast to help prevent fleas from jumping on your animals.

■ You can use natural insect repellents like Green Ban when you go out in the woods.

■ Read the warning labels on insecticides. What do they tell you?

There are about a million different kinds of insects that are known in the world! Some scientists think that there may be 30-50 million kinds of insects whom we haven't even discovered yet.

Keeping the Balance

Part of what makes Earth such an amazing planet is that lots of animals live here. Every animal has a place on the Earth, and they're all important, from the smallest fly to the biggest whale. That's why it's very foolish to kill animals just because we don't like them or understand their purpose. You already know how dangerous it can be to use insecticides to kill insects. People have messed up the whole planet because we've killed so many animals.

Get Some Facts!

■ Whenever people decide that they don't like certain animals and then try to get rid of them, they practically always create a worse problem.

■ People in Wyoming were having problems because prairie dogs were eating their crops. They started killing all the prairie dogs. But prairie dogs are the main food for black-footed ferrets. Guess what happened? That's right, the ferrets died too, and now there are almost no black-footed ferrets left in the world.

■ People have killed almost all the wolves and mountain lions and bobcats because these animals were thought to threaten cows and sheep on ranches. But wolves and big cats usually ate wild animals (like deer and elk) and helped to keep the balance. Believe it or not, our government actually spends more money killing wild animals who might harm farm animals than the cost of the farm animals who are killed by wild animals!

■ It's not just killing animals which messes up the balance. When rabbits were brought to Australia, there were few natural predators. The rabbits multiplied and created a real problem for farmers by eating their crops.

Some Things You Can Do to Keep the Balance

■ Let nature be, and let animals be free.

Messing up the Balance

(You'll need as many friends for this game as you can find.)

1.
Pick a scene in nature - called an ecosystem (for example: the seashore, a pond in the woods, a desert, a rain forest).

2.
Read about that ecosystem in the library so you'll understand who and what lives in it, and how everything is connected.

3.
Have each kid choose a part to play in the ecosystem. You'll want to include lots of different plants, animals, the sun, wind and rain, night creatures and day creatures. One kid should be a human being.

4.
Figure out how all the parts fit together: who eats what? who lives where? who needs what to live? Ask a lot of questions until you understand how every being is connected to all the others.

5.
Act out the scene. (You can even act it out to music which is a lot of fun!)

6.

Have the human being pick one kind of animal or plant that she thinks of as a pest and remove that animal or plant from the scene.

7.

Stop the music and the action and have each being think very hard. How will losing this plant or animal affect you? If you can think of a way that losing the plant or animal will affect you, say so.

8.

If you die because of what's happening in the ecosystem, get up and leave the play.

9.

Every time a plant or animal dies or is affected by the changes in the ecosystem, think about how those changes will affect you.

10.

Who's left in the end? What did you learn about messing up nature?

No one knows just why wolves howl, but their howls are beautiful, eerie songs, which they sing mostly at night.

chapter **7**

Home, Home on The Range

We've talked about a lot of animals so far: animals who share our homes with us, and animals people eat, and animals people use to entertain, and animals in laboratories, and even animals people don't like. But we've only talked a little bit about wild animals, and there's a lot to say about wild animals and a lot to know about how we can help them.

When I was 11 years old I went to Africa with my family. We saw thousands and thousands of wild animals. We saw elephants, rhinoceroses, hippopotamuses, flamingos, gazelles, wildebeests, warthogs, lions, cheetahs, leopards, giraffes, monkeys, hyenas, storks, ostriches and many others, too.

There aren't as many animals in Africa now. Most of the chimpanzees and gorillas are gone. The elephants and rhinoceroses are quickly disappearing, and hardly anybody ever sees a kudu anymore.

One of the reasons why wild animals are disappearing is that people are killing them for ivory, or horns or other silly things. Another reason is that the human population is growing so much, and people are cutting down forests and taking over all the land on the Earth. This is happening not only in Africa, but also in the United States, Europe and most other places, so that there isn't much room left for the animals. There's another reason, too: people are polluting the Earth so badly that many animals are dying.

If wild animals don't get some help soon, there won't be many left. If you want to make sure that wild animals stick around on planet Earth, just turn the page ...

... and then go save some lives!

Building for Birds

One of the easiest ways to help wild animals is to help the ones who live near you. No matter where you live, even in the middle of the biggest city in the world, there are going to be birds nearby. Not only is it easy to help the birds, it's also a lot of fun because they'll stick around and let you watch them fly and hear them sing.

Get Some Facts!

■ Most baby song birds have to eat every 20 minutes from sunrise to sunset. That's one of the reasons why it can be very hard to raise an orphaned baby bird.

■ Some birds are vegetarians, like parrots and cockatoos. Other birds, like robins, eat worms and insects. Birds called raptors, such as owls, hawks and eagles, eat animals like mice, rabbits, and moles.

■ Owls have very special feathers which help them to fly almost soundlessly. That's good for owls, but not for mice, because owls can swoop down at night and catch a mouse before the mouse even hears the owl.

Some Things You Can Do for Birds

You can build for birds! Here's how:

Build a Bird Feeder

Bird feeder #1
You'll need:

☞ a spring water plastic jug

☞ scissors

☞ a small branch

☞ wire or sturdy string

☞ an adult to help you

☞ birdseed

1. Cut large square openings in the plastic jug on two sides opposite each other. (The bottom of the openings should be two inches from the bottom of the jug.)

2. Make two holes across from each other half way between the bottom of the square opening and the bottom of the jug. (See page 51 for a picture of this feeder.) These holes should be large enough for the small branch to fit through.

3. Cut two small holes across from each other at the top, underneath the cap on the jug. These will be for the wire or string to hang the feeder.

4. Fill the bottom of the feeder with birdseed.

5. Hang the feeder from a tree branch that you can reach easily.

6. You'll need to fill up the feeder with birdseed whenever it runs out.

7. It may take a couple of weeks before the birds find your feeder, so be patient!

Bird feeder #2
You'll need:

☞ pine cones

☞ peanut butter

☞ a knife to spread the peanut butter

☞ birdseed

☞ yarn

Use the knife to spread peanut butter all over the pine cones. Then dip the pine cones in birdseed and hang them on trees with the yarn. Lots of birds like peanut butter and birdseed.

Remember: If you build bird feeders, the birds will begin to expect the food. If you forget to feed the birds in winter, they can get very hungry. Birds need to eat a lot of food often, so keep the feeders full! The birds will show how much they appreciate your help by coming to visit everyday, especially on the snowiest, coldest days of winter.

Birds like to take baths, and that's really fun to watch so ...

Build a Bird Bath
You'll need:

☞ a big rubber or plastic dish, like the top of a plastic garbage can or the tray of a large, plastic planter

☞ a watering can or jar

☞ a good memory

Place the rubber dish outside where you can see it and dig a small area in the ground in which the dish can sit securely. (IMPORTANT: If dogs or cats wander around in the area, you're going to have to put the dish up high where the dogs and cats can't reach it and possibly harm the birds.) Fill the dish with clean water every day. In the winter, birds will drink the water. Use warm water so that it won't freeze as quickly.

Build a Bird Blind

You'll need:

- ☞ an adult to help you
- ☞ wood
- ☞ a hammer
- ☞ some nails
- ☞ maybe a saw

With an adult, build a small wall to sit behind and watch the birds. You'll need to make a hole in the wall just at eye level. Put the wall in front of all your bird feeders in a place where you like sitting. You might want to use a log to sit on. In the winter, you can bundle up in warm clothes and sit quietly watching all the birds come to visit and eat. Your bird blind will keep you hidden so the birds won't get scared and fly away.

■ Plant trees, shrubs and bushes in your backyard. Songbirds like to hide in bushes and nibble on berries.

■ If your cats go outside make sure to put a bell on their collars. The bell will warn birds that your cat is nearby so they can fly away before your cat catches them. In the spring and summer, you have to be very careful because that's when young birds are learning to fly. They practice on the ground for awhile, and your cat could catch them easily. (IMPORTANT: remember to make sure to get an elastic collar for your cat so that if she ever gets tangled in a branch, her collar will stretch, and she won't choke!)

■ If you see a baby bird who has fallen out of his nest, get an adult to help you put him back right away! If you can't reach the nest, you can make a temporary one out of a shoe box lined with soft grass and wedged in the crook of the tree. Look carefully at the bird though: the young birds, called fledglings, who are learning how to fly don't belong in their nest anymore. Their parents are close by watching them, so they don't need your help. Fledglings have lots of feathers and are almost as big as their parents.

Some birds fly thousands of miles each spring and autumn to the same spot. No one knows quite how they do it!

■ If you have sliding glass doors on your house, stick cut-outs of big birds like owls, hawks and eagles on the glass. The cut-outs will warn other birds not to fly near the glass doors.

Caring for Backyard Critters

Not only can you help birds, you can help plenty of other animals who visit your backyard. Maybe you haven't seen too many animals around your house, but they're there. Some of them come out at night, and some of them live underground, and some of them are very tiny. So get out your magnifying glass and make some new friends.

Get Some Facts!

- If you see raised trails crisscrossing your lawn they may be mole hills. Moles live underground and make tunnels all over the place.

- Rabbits like to come out and nibble on food especially early in the morning and late in the afternoon.

- Lots of backyard animals come out only at night, but some animals, like groundhogs, sneak out during the day. Keep your eyes open!

Some Things You Can Do for Backyard Critters

- Let part of your backyard grow wild with weeds and brush and tall grass. Animals love to hide and build houses in wild brush and grass.

- Plant a tree in your backyard with your parents. One tree can provide a home for lots of animals like birds and raccoons and squirrels and bugs and bats!

Moles eat lots of insects, so they can be helpful to have under your lawn.

- Plant raspberry, blueberry and blackberry patches for animals.

- Leave mole hills, ant hills and bee nests alone.

Keeping the Ocean in Motion

These days parts of the ocean are so polluted that people can't even swim in them! The fishes and dolphins and whales and coral and seals are getting very sick from all the pollution. Not only that, but people are killing lots of sea creatures including dolphins and whales. We'd better stop killing all the animals!

Get Some Facts!

■ When people throw out plastic bags or balloons, some of them wind up in the oceans. Turtles and other sea creatures mistake these plastic bags for food and may eat them and die.

■ Some tuna fish and dolphins swim together. No one knows why. There are tuna fishers who catch tuna fish with big, long nets. The nets also catch and kill thousands of dolphins every year.

■ When people throw away plastic six-pack holders some wind up in the ocean. Birds, fishes and other sea animals get their heads and bodies stuck in the rings and can die.

Some Things You Can Do to Keep the Ocean in Motion

■ Avoid using plastic. If you buy something at the store, you can carry it home in a book bag, canvas sack or in your hands. You can also tell the cashier to keep the bag because you're saving turtles and other sea creatures.

■ Cut up plastic, six-pack holders before throwing them away. Better yet, try to avoid buying drinks which come in plastic holders!

■ If you have a balloon, be sure not to let it go flying up in the air. You don't know where it's going to go, and it could wind up killing animals in the ocean. If your school is planning a balloon launch (where they'll let lots of helium balloons go up into the air), you can get your KAAT friends together and ask your teachers not to do the launch. You can explain that you don't want to pollute the sea and kill animals with a bunch of balloons. Earth Island Institute, a group listed in the "To Learn More" section at the end of the book, will send you information on balloons, and how they can harm the environment.

■ If you go to the beach, consider bringing a trash bag with you. Before you leave, you can take a walk along the beach and pick up trash.

■ If you see horseshoe crabs or starfish on the sand who need to be in the water, you can help them get in. You'll save their lives that way!

■ *Carefully* pick up fish hooks and lines on the beach and throw them away. You may want to use gloves. Never touch any needles on the beach. Let the lifeguards or health department take care of them.

■ You may have already decided that you don't want to eat fishes anymore, but if you do eat tuna fish, you can make sure that you don't buy the kind who have been caught by killing dolphins.

Kid Heroes

An elementary school class in California heard that dolphins were getting killed in the nets which catch tuna fish, and they got really mad. They protested and wrote letters and made phone calls and generally made a big fuss. Making a big fuss works. Lots of tuna companies have agreed not to buy tuna fish who were caught in the nets which also kill dolphins!

Let it Rain

Rain forests are very special places. There aren't too many of them on planet Earth, but they're very important for the world. Rain forests are filled with animals and plants and medicines and foods. When we take care of the rain forests, we're taking care of millions of animals and trees and nuts and berries.

Instead of taking care of the amazing rain forests, people are cutting down the trees in them. Once the trees are cut down, they're gone forever. Rain forests don't grow back the way some other forests do, because the soil in rain forests is not very fertile. The soil needs the plants and trees to continually nourish it so it can, in turn, nourish the plants and trees! Once all the trees and plants and animals are gone, the rain forests are gone forever.

Turtles who live in the ocean spend practically their whole lives in the sea, only coming on shore to lay their eggs. When the eggs hatch, the baby turtles crawl straight down the beach into the water by themselves.

One reason why people are destroying the rain forests is to get timber to build chairs and tables out of special rain forest wood. Another reason why people are destroying the rain forests is to graze cattle on the land for hamburgers, which are then sold in wealthier countries.

People don't need hamburgers, but we sure do need the rain forests.

Get Some Facts!

■ Since rain forest land becomes useless after the trees are all cut down, grazing cows doesn't make much sense. In fact, people are destroying the rain forests only to find out that after a few years, the grass doesn't grow, and the cows have nothing to eat.

■ Most of the rain forests are in Central and South America and Africa, but the hamburger meat is mostly sold in the United States, Europe and Japan. In other words, eating some hamburgers here in the United States is destroying rain forests in South America.

■ Thousands of kinds of animals and plants are becoming extinct every year because people are destroying the rain forests.

■ Lots of medicines come from plants in the rain forests. Once the rain forests are gone, we may not be able to discover many new medicines which could cure diseases.

■ Just like you can get sick and have a fever, the earth's temperature can also get too high. Chemicals and pollutants in the air can actually raise the temperature of the earth, but trees can help keep the earth's temperature stable.

■ In the time it's taken you to read this chapter several acres of rain forest have been destroyed.

Some Things You Can Do to Save Rain Forests

■ Save cows and rain forests! You can avoid eating in fast food restaurants which may get some of their beef from rain forest-raised cows. (Most of the fast food hamburger restaurants will say that they don't buy beef from rain forest-raised cattle, but when beef from the rain forests arrives in the United States it is usually mixed with United States-raised beef, and it's all labeled U.S. beef. That makes it hard to know what beef is from the rain forests.)

■ Avoid getting rain forest wood, like teak, mahogany or rosewood. If you want something made out of wood, you can make sure the wood comes from trees nearby, not from the rain forests.

■ Write a report on the rain forests for school and let all your friends know how they can save the rain forests, too.

Write a Rain Forest Play

Write a play about the rain forest. The characters can be all the animals who live in the rain forests, plus the trees and the plants, the rain itself, and all the people who are destroying the forests. Put the play on for your friends and families and show everyone what's happening.

Kid Hero

A nine year old boy in Sweden heard about what was happening to the rain forests and wondered what he could do to save the trees, the waterfalls, and all the animals in the rain forests. He and his classmates decided to raise money to buy land in the forests. They called their land the Children's Eternal Forest. Now there are kids all over the world who are donating money to the Children's Eternal Forest to buy more land and save more trees and animals. If you want, you can donate money, too! You can have a bake sale at school or set up a lemonade stand and then you can give the money you raise to the Children's Eternal Rainforest, Monteverde Conservation League, Apartado 10165-1000, San José, Costa Rica.

Every year thousands of kinds of animals and plants disappear forever as the rain forests are destroyed.

Be a Garbage Rejector

How much trash do you think each person throws away in the United States everyday? One pound? Two pounds? Half a pound? Well the answer is four pounds every day! There's very little space left to put the trash anymore. So some people are burning it which can create very poisonous gases and ash, and some people are dumping the ashes into the ocean, and some people are trying to get rid of it by giving it to other countries. The fact is, there's no good way to get rid of so much garbage.

Garbage comes in different forms and shapes. When we pollute the Earth with chemicals, that's garbage; when we drive our cars and pollute the air, that's garbage, too.

What does garbage have to do with animals? People are turning the Earth into a big garbage can, and that's not good for people or animals. All the garbage is making the earth and the animals sick. We've got to clean up our act!

Get Some Facts!

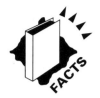

- Pollution from cars mixes with clouds and causes the rain to be polluted. It's called acid rain. Acid rain kills trees. Without the trees, the wild animals die, too.

- Believe it or not, there are a lot of garbage problems caused by paper. First of all, paper comes from trees. If paper is not recycled, that means a tree was cut down to make it. Bleaching paper to make it white often releases dangerous chemicals which sometimes get into the water (and which can also stay in the paper). Finally, people throw out so much paper that there's more paper in garbage dumps than anything else.

- Polystyrene (sometimes called Styrofoam) is the light, usually white material often used for hot drinks or packaging at take-out restaurants, for trays in school, or for packing fragile objects to send in the mail. Polystyrene is bad for the environment because it releases chemicals which harm the ozone layer in our atmosphere. The ozone layer protects us, animals and plants from the harmful rays of the sun.

- Using electricity, gas or oil in homes and buildings causes pollution.

Some Things You Can Do to Clean up the Mess

- Reuse and recycle everything you can! That includes paper, bottles and cans. You can call your local recycling center to find out what kinds of plastics you can recycle. You may want to organize KAAT members to collect trash to be recycled.

- You can avoid buying things made of plastic or polystyrene, or packaged in these materials.

- Food can even be recycled. Food recycling is called composting. Here's how to compost your food to make rich soil for your garden:

1.

Whenever you have food scraps left over from dinner put them in a large container. Never put animal products in your compost though. The container should be closed, but not so tightly that no air can get inside.

2.

Once a week, empty the container into an even larger container which you keep outside in a corner of your yard. The container can be a simple wire square, rectangle or circle, or an open wooden crate. You can actually compost without any container at all, just by making a pile of leaves and food garbage! The area should be at least 3 feet by 3 feet.

3.

Layer your food garbage with leaves, grass clippings and yard waste.

4.

Stir the contents of the container every couple of weeks.

5.

Watch the food turn into soil.

6.

Use the soil in your garden!

■ Instead of asking for a ride somewhere, you can ride a bike, walk or take public transportation. This protects the atmosphere from the pollution of so many cars.

■ If your school uses polystyrene trays in the cafeteria, you can talk to your teachers about switching to reusable trays. Students in New Jersey got their schools to make the switch!

Animals recycle! Birds will build nests using yarn, string, hair and other thrown out things which they find.

■ When you see people treating the Earth like a garbage can and throwing litter on the ground, you can pick their litter up, go to them and politely say "Excuse me, you dropped this." Then, hand it back to them! (Remember to be careful and friendly when you approach people you don't know.)

■ You can buy recycled paper and write on both sides of it. Don't waste any space!

Don't Trash Your Trash

(You'll need a couple of friends for this game.)

Bring out your trash cans and put them in the center of the room. Make sure that you don't have any food waste or used tissues or sharp objects in the cans. Have everyone close their eyes and reach in and pick out something from the trash. Discuss what the trash could be used for, instead of throwing it out. (For example, small jars can be used to make pencil holders, boxes can be used to wrap gifts, and cardboard can be used for artwork.) Keep doing this until you've emptied the trash cans. On one side pile up all the things which could be used for something else; on the other side pile up the things which can't be used for anything at all. Which side is bigger? Now that you know, start using your trash!

Spending for Animals

People buy a lot of things. Some of the things people buy are important, but some of them are not important at all, like lots and lots of toys or knick knacks. You already know that some things which people buy hurt animals (like fur coats). But did you know that every time you spend your money you could be affecting animals too? That's why it's important to be an animal sleuth whenever you go shopping.

Get Some Facts!

■ When people buy more than they need, more garbage is produced. More garbage means more pollution, which means more sick animals and a sick Earth.

■ Wild animal parts find their way into all sorts of things people buy.

■ The better a toy is made, the better it is for the Earth and animals. Poorly made toys which fall apart quickly or get thrown out hurt animals and the Earth.

■ Plastic toys stay on the Earth for a long, long time. They don't disintegrate like stuffed animals or other cloth toys to become part of the soil.

How You Can Spend for Animals

■ Avoid buying toys that are poorly made or are made with lots of plastic.

■ Try to buy only what you really want or need.

■ Make your own toys from nature. You can make wind chimes with shells or pebbles and string, or paint pine cones or rocks, or press flowers in a book, or design sculptures with dead wood.

If aliens come visit planet Earth in a thousand years, they'll find plastic dolls and guns and bags and cups and balls all over the place. What do you suppose they'll think of that?

Here's how to make the wind chimes:
You'll need:

☞ pebbles or shells or wood pieces
which you've collected from the ground

☞ very thin string or wire

☞ a small tree branch

☞ scissors

1.
Use the thread or wire and wrap it around the pebbles, shells or wood pieces.

2.
Knot the string so that the pebbles or shells are held firmly in place.

3.
Tie string or wire to the pebbles, shells or wood pieces and wrap the other end around the small branch so that the pebbles, shells or pieces of wood hang close together. (Hang the strings so that they are pretty close together, too.) If you want, you can paint the branch.

4.
Use the string or wire to hang the branch outside in the wind.

5.
Listen when the wind blows.

■ Have a toy, clothes and book trading party! Invite your friends over and tell them to bring the things that they don't want anymore. When everyone gets to your house, start trading your toys and clothes. You'll come away with great stuff, and you won't have hurt the earth or animals at all!

■ Ask your parents if they will buy recycled products. You can even get recycled toilet paper and tissues from food cooperatives, natural food stores and mail-order catalogues!

Protecting City Wildlife

Most animals need grass and trees and earth to live, but some animals manage to live in the middle of big cities. Can you think of some of them?

Get Some Facts!

- Pigeons and mourning doves build nests in the corners and on ledges of big buildings.

- Some rats make their homes in sewers, basements and underground structures like subway stations.

- Mice will make their homes in between the walls of apartments.

- Worms live in the soil in little tree planters on the sidewalk.

Some Things You Can Do for City Animals

■ Go to the park and feed the pigeons birdseed. If you see one pigeon and start feeding her, you're bound to be surrounded by pigeons in a few minutes!

■ If you have a mouse in your apartment remember to use the mouse house to catch him without killing him. You'll have to take him to a park when it's warm to let him go.

■ If you see people hurting an animal on the street, get an adult to help you stop them.

■ There are lots of people who live in cities, so if you're walking around the street you're probably going to pass people all the time. That's the perfect time to be wearing your "Save the Animals" t-shirt or your "Fur Hurts" button because a lot of people will see it!

When pigeons walk they have to move their heads back and forth. This helps pigeons see things clearly.

Save Some Room

Because people are taking all the animals' land away from them, there are a lot of animals who are in trouble. They're getting hit by cars, and caught in tractors, and trapped in attics, and orphaned when their moms are killed. Life can be pretty hard for animals now that there's so little room for them.

Get Some Facts!

■ Every time a new mall or housing development goes up, trees are cut down and the soil is all cut up. All the animals who lived in those trees and in that earth have to move. But there's hardly anywhere for them to go because there's so little room left!

■ When people build roads, the roads may cut right through a forest or field. The animals still want to get from one side to the other, but now, when they cross the road, they can get hit and killed by cars.

■ About 350 million animals are hit and killed by cars every year in the United States. That's about 1 million animals each day!

Some Things You Can Do to Help Save Some Room

■ Ask your parents not to drive faster than the speed limit. By driving slower, there's less of a chance of hitting animals. Be especially careful when driving at night. Driving less often is also a good idea because then you'll protect animals and the environment.

■ Call the SPCA or animal shelter or look in the telephone book to find out the names and phone numbers of local wildlife rehabilitators. Wildlife rehabilitators are the people who rescue and care for wild animals who have been hit by cars, shot, injured or who have been orphaned. Ask if you can visit them. Perhaps you can volunteer to help take care of injured and orphaned animals. That would help animals and be a lot of fun at the same time.

■ If you see an animal who's been injured, and it is safe to help the animal, get an adult to help you bring the animal to the wildlife rehabilitators. (Never pick up an injured animal yourself. The animal may be sick, or may bite you!)

■ Plant a special garden for wildlife, but fence in your own garden so you'll both have food.

■ IMPORTANT: Only do this if it is safe! If you see an animal who has been killed on the road, get an adult to help you move the animal off the road with a big stick. The reason for moving the animal is this: dead animals on the road may attract other animals who could get hit by cars, too.

Some towns have put passageways under roads so that wild animals can get from one side of the road to the other without getting hit by cars.

■ Never, ever throw food out the window of a car. The food will attract animals to the road, and then they may get hit and killed by cars.

■ If people buy fewer things from stores, then there won't be as many stores. If you and your friends don't buy things you don't need, then maybe the new mall or shopping center won't be built! Then there will be more room for animals.

Kid Hero

When Diane was nine years old she volunteered at a wildlife sanctuary in New Jersey. She cleaned the cages, and fed the baby birds (who needed to eat every twenty minutes) and kept the animals warm and happy. Sometimes she got up very early on Sunday mornings in the middle of winter to come to the sanctuary and help the animals. She'd fill up their bowls with warm water and break the ice in the pond for the ducks.

chapter

8

Show You Care

Night and day
from June to May
with what you say
and how you play
you can save animals everyday.
Everyday in every way!

Learn and Share

We're almost at the end, but I've saved some of the best stuff for last. You've learned about a lot of the things that are happening to animals, and you've learned how you can help animals, but just as important as learning from this book is learning from the animals themselves, and then sharing what you've learned with your family and friends.

I'd like you to go on a couple of adventures to get to know animals. Here's the first one:

KAAT Adventure #1
The Scavenger Hunt

This scavenger hunt is different from most scavenger hunts because you're not going to pick up, touch or bother anything or anyone. Take a pad and pencil and write down where you see things. It's most fun to do this with friends, but you can do it alone, too.

Get out your binoculars and magnifying glass and go find:

☞ a feather

☞ some fur

☞ the remains of an animal

☞ a leaf that's been eaten by an animal

☞ an animal home above you

☞ an animal home below you

☞ an animal home at eye level

☞ animal droppings

☞ a reptile (like a snake, lizard or turtle)

☞ a mammal (any animal with fur)

☞ a bird

☞ an amphibian (like a toad, frog, newt or salamander)

☞ an animal who eats other animals

☞ an animal who eats plants

☞ animal tracks

☞ a worm

☞ an insect

When you've found everything, or almost everything, come back and meet with your friends. Tell each other everything you saw and share what you learned.

Now here's the second one:

KAAT Adventure #2
The Wonder Watch

You'll need:

☞ a pad and pencil

☞ paints or crayons

Go to the woods, or an open field, or a pond or the beach, and find a spot where you can be all by yourself. Sit. Just sit. Don't move, don't fidget, don't wander, don't play, just sit. And listen, and stare, and smell, and feel the earth beneath you, and the breeze on your skin, and the temperature of the air, and the feelings in your own body. And wait. And sit some more.

I'm not going to tell you about the great things that will happen. You can find that out on your own. If and when you feel like it, take out your pad and pencil, or your paints and crayons, and draw and paint or write poems about sitting by yourself on the earth with all the animals and plants around you. Later, when you go home, share your drawings and poems with someone you really love.

■ Once you get to know the earth and all the animals, you may want to tell everybody how important it is to help save them. If you've been waiting to do some of the activities to help animals, now's the time to make lots of posters for animals, and write songs to sing, and plays to act, and t-shirts to wear. Now's the time to let everyone know what's happening to animals.

What's Happenin'

(You'll need a friend for this role play.)

Choose one kid to talk about what's happening to animals, and the other to listen and learn. Practice sharing your love and concern for animals until you really feel that you can tell people why it's so important to help animals. Switch roles and practice again. Once you're good at it, go talk to your friends and family.

Be Aware

In order to save animals you need to be aware. That means you have to keep your detective eyes on, and think about your actions, and keep your ears open all the time.

How to Help Animals Everyday in Every Way

■ Keep an animal notebook. Write down everything you think, see, learn, feel or hear about animals. You can also write down your ideas and feelings about KAAT activities, skits, and games, or about any of the things you've learned or felt reading this book.

■ When you go to sleep at night, think about your whole day and remember how the things you did had a connection with animals, whether through food, or clothing, or with your dog, cat or hamster, or with wildlife. Before you go to sleep, think about whether you helped animals that day. If you want to help animals even more, you can decide to do something new for animals in the morning.

■ Examine your beliefs: figure out when you think it's okay to hurt or kill animals and when it's not. You may find that your beliefs change as you get older. You may find that some of your beliefs changed just from reading this book! It's always important to examine your beliefs so do this activity every month or so.

■ If your beliefs change, you can change your behavior, too! If you decide it's wrong to kill animals when you don't absolutely have to, then you can make sure that you aren't responsible for animals being killed.

■ No one likes to be told what to do, but most people like to live by their principles and beliefs. You can help animals by helping your friends figure out their beliefs, too. In fact, why not tell five friends about what you've learned in this book. You can ask them to tell five friends, too. Spreading the word will help animals a lot. And don't forget to share your thoughts and feelings with your parents.

■ If you see animals who need help, help them. And remember, humans are animals too!

■ Try not to contribute to animal suffering. That's hard because animals suffer so much for so many things, and it's not always easy to stop doing things that hurt animals. You can try really hard though, right? If certain chickens are suffering to lay eggs, you can buy eggs from happier chickens or not buy eggs at all. If an animal suffers in a zoo, you don't have to go to that zoo. Visit the woods instead. If an animal suffered to test some product, you can buy a different product instead. Just stay aware and show you care.

Take the Dare

A KAAT Animal Council

In this last KAAT activity you will hold an animal council. Holding an animal council is very serious business. Only kids who truly want to help animals should participate in the animal council, because if you participate, you've taken the biggest dare of all. You've made a solemn promise to help animals. And promises like that must never be broken. So gather some friends together who really want to save animals, and hold an animal council. Here's how:

You'll need:

-  a quiet place in the woods or in a room where you won't be disturbed
- construction paper, paints, crayons
- stones, shells or other important objects
- scissors
- glue
- any other art supplies that you have
- about an hour of time when you won't be disturbed

Choosing the Organizer and Explaining the Council

Gather around in a circle and choose one person to be the organizer. The organizer should be the person most acquainted with the procedures. She or he will be keeping track of time and making sure that all the parts of the council go smoothly. The organizer will also explain the procedures to all the kids.

Procedures

1.

Each person should find a quiet spot to be alone. Sit or lie down so that you are comfortable. Close your eyes, and let the image of an animal come to you. Don't force yourself to think about a certain animal; let the animal visit you in your thoughts.

2.

Pretend that you are the animal. What does the animal have to say to you? Ask yourself questions like "What is happening to me as this animal?" "How do I feel?" "What do I want?" "What do I have to say?" Listen inside for the answers.

3.

When you are ready, get up and go to the art supplies and using whatever is there, construct a mask to represent yourself as the animal. The mask does not have to look like the animal as long as it feels like it represents the animal to you.

4.

When everyone is done making their mask, come into the circle again. The organizer should call people together and ask all the animals who have come to the council to speak.

5.

One by one each animal should introduce him or herself, and say what is happening in the world that is hurting him or her. After each animal speaks, the council should respond by saying "we hear you." For example, if a pig speaks and talks about how she is put into a dark, crowded building and can't turn around or be with her babies, the council will respond by saying "we hear you, pig." Continue around the circle until every animal has spoken and has been heard.

6.

The organizer should then ask the animals to each speak again, this time telling the council what they have to offer, what makes them special, or what qualities are worthy of respect and care. The rest of the animals respond by saying, "we thank you." For example, the pig might say "I give you intelligence and playfulness," and the rest of the animals say "we thank you, pig."

7.

After each has spoken again, the organizer should ask the animals to talk once more, saying what they want human beings to do to help. The rest of the animals respond by saying "we hear you." For example, the pig might say "I want people to stop eating me," and the other animals would respond, "we hear you, pig."

8.

Finally, after each animal has said what they want and need from people, the organizer should ask the participants to take off their masks one by one. As each of you takes off your mask, you will make your solemn promise to change one aspect of your behavior which hurts the animal you spoke for. For example, the person who has represented the pig may promise to eat less bacon and ham, or perhaps not to eat pigs anymore.

9.

The organizer should remind each participant that the promises are very serious, and no promise should be made that can't be kept. A small promise kept is far better than a big promise broken.

10.

The council ends when the organizer says something like: "These promises made shall not be broken. Many thanks to the animals who have come together today to share their feelings, dreams, hopes and wisdom."

11.

When the council is over, the organizer should ask each participant if they would be willing to meet again. Those who wish to meet again should schedule another time for holding an animal council. You may find that each council becomes easier and more meaningful.

12.

As you leave, know that you are helping animals and making the world a better place for all creatures. Remind yourself that you can save animals' lives and end animal suffering.

To Learn More

There are a lot of different groups and organizations which will help you save animals. Some will send you information, or magazines, and some will give you ideas or supply you with posters and flyers. Don't by shy about calling these groups. They want to hear from you and help you in any way they can.

Groups for Kids

Animalearn 801 Old York Rd., #204, Jenkintown, PA 19046-1685 (215) 887-0816. This is the group that I'm from, and I would be really happy to hear from you! We offer student guides, materials for school projects, classes and presentations in our own region, summer programs and youth empowerment workshops.

Dissection Hotline If you don't want to dissect animals in school you can call: 1-800-922-FROG. They'll help you out!

Humane Education Committee P.O. Box 445, New York, NY 10128 (212) 410-3095. This group will provide materials for your teachers, to help them teach you about animals. They'll also suggest some great books for you to read.

LivingEarth Learning Project 333 Washington St., Suite 850, Boston, MA 02108 (617) 523-6020. This group offers classes to students throughout New England and New York. They can also answer your questions and supply you with materials for school projects.

NAHEE (National Association for the Advancement of Humane and Environmental Education) P.O. Box 362, East Haddam, CT 06423 (203) 434-8666. This group will send your teacher a subscription to a magazine which will help teach you kids about kindness to animals.

Otterwise P.O. Box 1374, Portland, ME 04104. They print a newsletter just for kids!

PETA Kids (PETA stands for People for the Ethical Treatment of Animals) P.O. Box 42516, Washington, DC 20015 (301) 770-7444. PETA Kids is a newsletter just for young people!

SACA (Student Action Corps for Animals) P.O. Box 15588, Washington, DC 20003-0588 (202) 543-8983. If you want to find out about other "kind kids" near you or get advice, SACA can help. They can also help if you don't want to dissect animals in school.

Vegetarian Education Network (VE•Net) P.O. Box 3347, West Chester, PA 19381 (717) 529-8638. VE•Net provides information and support to young vegetarians and helps with school lunches. They also publish *How on Earth!*, a magazine written by and for young people who are involved in the animal rights, environmental and/or vegetarian movements, and sponsor Youth Empowerment Workshops.

Groups Which Will Send You Lots of Information and Flyers

American Anti-Vivisection Society 801 Old York Rd., #204, Jenkintown, PA 19046-1685 (215) 887-0816.

American Humane Association 63 Inverness Dr. East, Englewood, CO 80112 (303) 792-9900.

ASPCA 441 E. 92nd St., New York, NY 10128 (212) 876-7700.

Animal Protection Institute P.O. Box 22505, Sacramento, CA 95822 (916) 731-5521.

Friends of Animals P.O. Box 1244, Norwalk, CT 06856, (203) 866-5223.

Fund for Animals 200 W. 57th St., New York, NY 10019 (212) 246-2096.

Humane Society of the United States 2100 L St. NW, Washington, DC 20037 (202) 452-1100.

In Defense of Animals 816 W. Francisco Blvd., San Rafael, CA 94901 (415) 453-0510.

International Fund for Animal Welfare P.O. Box 193, Yarmouth Port, MA 02675 (508) 362-6268.

International Society for Animal Rights 421 S. State St., Clarks Summit, PA 18411 (717) 586-2200.

Last Chance for Animals 18653 Ventura Blvd., Tarzana, CA 91356 (818) 760-2075/8340.

National Anti-Vivisection Society 53 W. Jackson Blvd. Suite 1550, Chicago, IL 60604 (312) 427-6065.

New England Anti-Vivisection Society 333 Washington St., Suite 850, Boston, MA 02108 (617) 523-6020.

PETA (People for the Ethical Treatment of Animals) P.O. Box 42516, Washington, DC 20015 (301) 770-7444.

Progressive Animal Welfare Society (PAWS) P.O. Box 1037, Lynnwood, WA 98046 (206) 742-4142.

Groups of Doctors and Scientists
Who Can Help You

Association of Veterinarians for Animal Rights P.O. Box 6269, Vacaville, CA 95696 (707) 451-1391.

Medical Research Modernization Committee P.O. Box 6036 Grand Central Station, New York, NY 10163-6018 (212) 876-1368.

Physicians Committee for Responsible Medicine 5100 Wisconsin Ave. Suite 404, Washington, DC 20016 (202) 686-2210.

Psychologists for the Ethical Treatment of Animals P.O. Box 1297, Washington Grove, MD 20880-1297 (301) 963-4751.

Groups Which Help Farm Animals

Farm Animal Reform Movement P.O. Box 70123, Washington, DC 20088 (301) 530-1737.

Farm Sanctuary P.O. Box 150, Watkins Glen, NY (607) 583-2225. They actually rescue abused cows, sheep, pigs, turkeys, ducks, geese and chickens. You can help these animals by adopting some or by paying for their food each year. If you live nearby, go and visit. It's great for kids!

Humane Farming Association 1550 California St., Suite 6, San Francisco, CA 94109 (415) 485-1495.

United Poultry Concerns P.O. Box 59367, Potomoc, MD 20859 (301) 948-2406. This group is concerned with teaching about and protecting chickens, turkeys, geese and ducks.

Groups Which Help Dolphins and Whales

Earth Island Institute 300 Broadway, Suite 28, San Francisco, CA 94133 (415) 788-3666.

Greenpeace 1611 Connecticut Ave. NW, Washington, DC 20009 (202) 462-1177.

Sea Shepherd Conservation Society P.O. Box 7000, S. Redondo Beach, CA 90277 (213) 373-6979.

Groups Which Help Monkeys and Apes

International Primate Protection League P.O. Box 766, Summerville, SC 29484 (803) 871-2280.

Primarily Primates P.O. Box 15306, San Antonio, TX 78212-8506 (512) 755-4616.

Groups Which Help Dogs and Cats

Call your local pound, animal shelter, humane society or SPCA.

Groups Which Help the Environment

EarthSave Foundation 706 Frederick St., Santa Cruz, CA 95062-2205 (408) 423-4069.

Greenpeace 1611 Connecticut Ave., NW, Washington, DC 20009 (202) 462-1177.

Rainforest Action Network 300 Broadway, San Francisco, CA 94133 (415) 398-4404.

Some Great Books to Read

(Some of these books you may find in bookstores, but others will only be in libraries.)

Cockleburr Quarters by Charlotte Baker. New York: Prentice Hall, Inc., 1972.

Jenny's Corner by Frederic Bell. New York: Random House, 1974.

The Incredible Journey by Sheila Burnford. Bantam Books, 1977.

Mustard by Charlotte Graeber. New York: McMillan, 1982.

Much Ado About Aldo by Johanna Hurwitz. New York: William Morrow, 1978.

Aldo Applesauce by Johanna Hurwitz. New York: William Morrow, 1979.

Bambi by Felix Salten. New York: Simon & Schuster, 1988.

Blood in the Snow by Marlene Fanta Shyer. Boston: Houghton Mifflin: 1975.

Storm Boy by Colin Thiele. New York: Harper & Row, 1963.

JT by Jane Wagner. New York: Van Nostrand Reinhold Co., 1969.

Charlotte's Web by E.B. White. New York: Dell Publishing Co., 1952.

Finding Fever by Thomas Baird. New York: Harper & Row, 1982.

Seal Secret by Aidan Chamers. New York: Harper & Row, 1980.

Julie of the Wolves by Jean Craighead George. New York: Harper & Row, 1972.

The Talking Earth by Jean Craighead George. New York: Harper & Row, 1987.

Grip by Helen Griffiths. New York: Holiday House, 1978.

Just a Dog by Helen Griffiths. New York: Holiday House, 1974.

The Greyhound by Helen Griffiths. New York: Doubleday & Co., 1964.

Gentle Ben by Walt Morey. New York: Avon, 1976.

Alan and the Animal Kingdom by Isabelle Holland. New York: Lippincott, 1977.

50 Simple Things Kids Can Do To Save The Earth by the Earthworks Group. New York: Andrews & McMeel, 1990.

Kids Can Save the Animals by Ingrid Newkirk, available from PETA.

Animals' Agenda P.O. Box 25881, Baltimore, MD 21224. This is a magazine all about animals.

Vegetarian Cookbooks and Books about Vegetarianism

Simply Vegan by Debra Wasserman. Baltimore, Maryland: Vegetarian Resource Group, 1991.

Kids Can Cook: Vegetarian Recipes Kitchen-Tested by Kids for Kids by Dorothy Bates. Tennessee: Book Publishing Company, 1987.

Burgers 'n Fries 'n Cinnamon Buns by Bobbie Hinman. P.O. Box 8100, Newark, Delaware, 19714-8100: Bobbie Hinman, 1992.

How to Eat Without Meat by Judy and Shari Zucker. From American Vegan Society, 501 Old Harding Highway, Malaga, NJ 08328 (609) 694-2887.

Going Vegetarian: A Guide for Teenagers by Sada Fretz. New York: William Morrow, 1983.

Pregnancy, Children and the Vegan Diet by Michael Klaper, M.D. Hawaii: Gentle World, 1987.

Diet for a New America by John Robbins. New Hampshire: Stillpoint Publishing, 1987.

Bye, for Now

Now that you know how much there is that you can do to save animals, you're probably going to be very busy. You might want to share this book with some friends so that they can help you.

I'd really like to hear any stories you and your friends have about helping animals. If you let me know, I can tell other kids about what you've done. It's great to share ideas. So if you have a story or a drawing or an idea, you can send it to me at:

Animalearn
801 Old York Road, #204
Jenkintown, PA 19046-1685

Good luck, have fun, and ...

... keep saving lives!

your friend,

Zoe Weil

If you enjoyed
So, You Love Animals,
share it with a friend!

To order additional copies, please use the form below.

Also available from Animalearn:

Animals in Society: Facts and Perspectives on Our Treatment of Animals, by Zoe Weil, the first book about animal issues for secondary school students. Filled with photographs, projects and resources.

Animals in Society
By Zoe Weil
$4.95 each
plus shipping

For five or more copies call for special rates:
1-800-SAY-AAVS

Send coupon and check made payable to AAVS to:

*Animalearn/AAVS
801 Old York Road, #204
Jenkintown, PA
19046-1685*

For 1–4 copies:

Please send me _____ copies of *Animals in Society* at $4.95 each ($5.95 each in Canada) plus $2.00 shipping and handling for first copy, $.50 each additional copy.

Please send me _____ copies of *So, You Love Animals* at $12.95 each ($14.95 each in Canada) plus $2.00 shipping and handling for first copy, $.50 each additional copy.

Books will be shipped UPS, so please use a street address, not a P.O. Box.

Name: _____

Address: _____

_____

Total Enclosed: _____

P.A. residents please add 6% sales tax.